The Blacksmith of Fallbrook

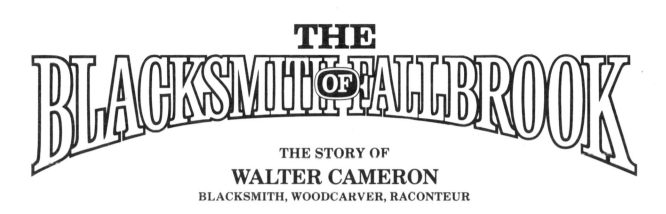

THE BLACKSMITH OF FALLBROOK

THE STORY OF
WALTER CAMERON
BLACKSMITH, WOODCARVER, RACONTEUR

Audrey Armstrong

MUSSON BOOK COMPANY
a division of General Publishing Co. Ltd.
Don Mills, Ontario

First published in 1979 by
Musson Book Company
a division of
General Publishing Co. Ltd.
30 Lesmill Road, Don Mills, Ontario

First printing

Canadian Cataloguing in Publication Data
Armstrong, Audrey I., 1920 —
    The Blacksmith of Fallbrook

ISBN 0-7737-1050-2

1. Cameron, Walter, 1894-   2. Blacksmiths —
Ontario — Fallbrook — Biography.   3. Fallbrook,
Ontario — Biography.   I. Title.

FC3099.F35A75   971.3'82'00924   C79-094080-9
F1059.5.F35A75

The film mentioned on p. 80 is *Knacky People*, directed
by Gary Nicol, distributed by Viking Films Ltd., 525
Denison Street, Markham, Ontario L3R 1B8

Printed and bound in Canada
Book and cover design by Maher & Murtagh
Photographs on cover and on pp. 4, 21, 39, 41, 43, 44, 49,
51, 64, 74, 77, 79, 82, 83, 97
by John Murtagh

Contents

Author's Introduction

"Walter," I said to my friend Walter Cameron one day, "do you realize you are an octogenarian?" "Well, by golly, maybe I am," he chuckled, "I've been just about everything else!"

Walter Cameron has lived in the tiny village of Fallbrook, in eastern Ontario, since his birth in 1894. He grew up in a house next door to his blacksmith father's shop, the product of a loving, gregarious mother and a stern and taciturn Scottish father. The result was a philosopher-blacksmith with a strong sense of humour and history. He joined his father in the smithy at the age of sixteen and still spends many hours working there. Although the days are over when he delighted in taking on the district's most difficult horses to shoe or repairing sometimes almost irreparable machinery to keep farmers in operation for miles around, he can be found, most days, in the old blacksmith shop. Walter still enjoys hammering out trivets and ox and horseshoes for souvenirs over his forge and working at his carvings in his adjoining wood-working shop.

Thousands of people have visited the Cameron blacksmith shop in Fallbrook to see this monument to an older way of life and to talk to the man who personifies the history of the neighbourhood. Classes of schoolchildren, busloads of tourists, or friends in ones and twos stop by for a few minutes or a few hours to hear Walter's stories of times gone by and to watch him work at his forge. A historian and raconteur of his skill is also in great demand as a speaker to groups and as a demonstrator at fairs and exhibitions. Walter Cameron has earned the title of Lanark's Living Legend.

Over the years my family and I have enjoyed countless conversations with Walter and I have come to feel that his story deserves to be much more widely known. I hope that the many who cannot visit him in Lanark County will catch the flavour of Walter's conversation and relive some of the history of the area where for many years life revolved around his shop.

Audrey Armstrong

1
Ancestral Ties and Tales

You know, they say that people were smaller a century or so ago, but my grandfather was six feet, five-and-a-half inches; they called him Long John, that could have been the reason! And they had to be sturdy. In those days it was the survival of the fittest.

Oh, I tell you, I just worship some of those old people, the things they did. When I pass their graves I take off my hat to them. Just to exist was a hardship in those days.

The Cameron Family

My grandfather was a farmer at Lachute, Quebec and he had a big family — eight boys and five girls. He died in 1897 of cancer; his doctor had told him what it was and what that

man suffered was something terrible. Nothing much to relieve the pain in those days, you know. After he died — oh, I was about three years old — I can remember watching a little white cloud up in the sky and telling my mother I could see Grandpa up there.

My father, James Cameron, started out to look for work when he was a young lad. He came from Lachute up to Ottawa and out to the big McKellar farm on the Richmond Road. There's a radio station there now but it would have been outside Ottawa then. He asked for work on the farm and Mr. McKellar said, oh, he had lots of men, lots of men. They milked about fifty cows at the dairy farm there; that was a lot in those days; kept four men and they got up at three in the morning to get the cows milked and the milk on the street before breakfast time.

"Well," Father asked, "what are you paying?" "Eleven dollars a month, but we don't need anybody, don't need anybody — have all the help we need." And as my father was turning to leave the man said, "What did you say your name was?" "Cameron, James Cameron." "Are you by any chance related to Watty Cameron?" "Watty Cameron's my brother," and he hired him on the spot. What one brother did for the other! Oh, a terror!

Later on Father went back to Lachute to work as a blacksmith, to serve his apprenticeship with his brother, William. Uncle Will had learned the blacksmithing trade at Lachute and then Father learned from him. In those days Father and his brother built the ploughs and harrows for the farmers. I've got a set of drag harrows over in the old shop that they made, oh, years and years ago.

Uncle Will was a blacksmith and a good one but he took a notion to go to Colorado to the Gold Rush there and then Father came up to Ontario again as blacksmith in McLaren's Supply Depot. You see McLaren's was the supply centre for the shanties, the lumber camps.

Oh, I guess the old timers had a terrible time at those lumber camps. Hard to keep themselves clean, you know. When my father worked at McLaren's Depot as blacksmith, the bed bugs were so bad they had to leave the lamps lit all night; the bed bugs won't come out with the light on, he said. My uncle Watty used to tell us that when he was at the shanty he

Walter's relations: Uncle Watty (with pipe) and Aunt Annie Cameron from Cote du Midi, Quebec

2

would get up first in the morning to get the towel while it was still clean.

Well, then, on the first of May, 1888, Father came here to Fallbrook; I guess his brother Watty in the hotel got him to come. You see Uncle Walter, Watty everybody called him, had the Farmers' Hotel here in Fallbrook; you'll see that in the Lanark County Atlas.

The blacksmith shop had been built back in 1865 by William Lees and a man by the name of Hunter was the first blacksmith. He made axes and did general work but he couldn't make a go of it and then Bob Clarke took over. He was a left-handed blacksmith; I've never seen a left-handed blacksmith working but he'd have to turn the anvil the other way — the horn to the right and work on it that way. Well, after a while John Buffam took over but he'd quit before Dad came. Father took over in 1888 and boarded up at Uncle Watty's hotel at the top of the hill.

My mother was a dressmaker before she was married. She'd travel around and stay at the homes where they needed some sewing. And she was back there making dresses for my Aunt Marjorie; that's how my father

Walter's mother, Margaret Matilda Cameron, in the early 1890s

and mother met.

They were married in January, 1891, and they moved into that house up on the hill, the blacksmith's house, the back part of it; that's all there

3

James Cameron, Walter's father, near the end of his life

was to it then. More was built onto it in later years. And, oh, my mother was a great woman; she helped Father go right ahead, helped everybody and got the thing going, and they stayed. It's been in Dad's name and mine for ninety-one years now. Have you ever noticed that a man or woman that's proud of their mother won't go far astray? I've watched that.

Mother had a great sense of humour, you know; she taught us all how to laugh. I used to tell her funny little stories that I'd heard at the shop or little things that happened, just to hear her laugh. She was a happy woman inside, self-secure. And Father was a serious man; never saw the funny side of anything in his life, a sober Scot.

Oh, Dad was looked up to in the community. He was fair, you know, but wouldn't stand for any foolishness. In the old days my father would go and sit up with a sick man or my mother would go and sit up with a sick woman; I've done it in my younger days too. They don't bother now.

You know I'm very proud of the work that my father could do. He came to Fallbrook with a good education in his craft. Uncle William was an excellent blacksmith and an expert at tempering steel and Father learned from him how to temper those old mill picks. He got a lot of this special work from the grist mills around. In the old days the stones that ground the grain and everything

A piece of a millstone, said to be a fragment of a meteor, and a mill pick made by Walter's father

got worn from rubbing against one another. The grooves had to be about the depth of a kernel of grain to work right. And Father used to make and grind the picks they used to make the grooves in the millstones. He had some chemical he kept in a two-gallon crock; he never told me what it was but he got that at the drugstore and he mixed it up. He would temper those mill picks and to test if he had got it tempered right he'd see if he could write his name on glass with it and the glass wouldn't break.

Oh, it was a very important job because those old millstones came from Scotland and they were harder than natural rock. They said they were made from old meteors that were dug up in Scotland. It was like a melted substance and it was

terrifically hard! I have some pieces in the shop.

Oh, it was a very particular business, tempering the mill picks. I know it was important because I lived around the old grist mill and I was in it hundreds of times, hundreds of times! I've seen them putting the grooves in and I've got a big inch-and-a-half screw that they used to use. They'd take that with the coarse thread on it and they'd lift the top stone up and hold it while they cut the bottom stone with the mill picks.

Before there were any grist mills in Lanark County, the old people, like my wife's grandfather, carried a bushel of wheat to Brockville and got it ground. That was fifty or sixty miles through the bush, both ways.

Well, Uncle William came back from the Gold Rush at Colorado, or wherever it was, and got married and when he was going back his brother, Hugh, the youngest lad — he was eighteen then — wanted to go with him. Oh, Hugh was a powerful man, a very powerful man. Uncle Watty told me one time that when he was thirty-five years old and Hugh Allan was eighteen he could tie knots in Uncle Watty, he was so much stronger.

5

Hugh Allan went to Colorado with Uncle Will to work in the mines. After a while he got to be boss and he got the reputation of being a pretty tough man. And in those days you had to prove it! One evening Uncle Will and Uncle Hugh were coming home with their dinner pails and somebody ran out and told Hugh that there was this big Swedish blacksmith up at the saloon, "and he says he's going to lick you tonight!" "What saloon did you say he was in?" Uncle Hugh asked and he handed his dinner pail to Uncle Will. Uncle Will said, "Well, you're not going alone," and away the two of them went.

There was this swinging door going into the bar and they could hear this lad telling everybody what he was going to do to Cameron when he met him. Uncle Hugh pushed open the door and somebody yelled, "There's Cameron!" The Swede took a swing at him and Uncle Hugh stepped to one side and hit the big lad and they say he broke his jaw in three places! In one swing!

Well, then he got in bad with somebody; he was foreman in the mine at this time and he used to be on the job first every morning. There

Walter Cameron's blacksmith uncle, William, from Lachute, Quebec, photographed in 1945

was an old mine shaft and they'd put a plank across the top and Hugh always walked across this to get to work. Somebody at night had sawed almost through the plank where he had to walk and he fell down through and broke his back.

I had a second cousin who went to the Cariboo Country when the Gold Rush was on there — John Cameron, with his wife, Sophia. He struck it rich and up there he was known as Cariboo Cameron. There's a story written about him, *The Cariboo Cameron Story*. His wife died while they were up there and they carried the coffin out over the trail. And they said he came out of there with eight pack horses loaded with gold, came home and set up four brothers with farms and machinery.

I never get tired of thinking of my uncle; his name was Walter Graham Cameron. His mother was Walter Graham's daughter and she married my grandfather, Long John Cameron. Their first son was Laughlan, a fine boy, quiet, he interfered with nobody. Well, he went to school in the old days when there wasn't much education for anybody. They had a drunken old soldier for a school master and when he was drunk he was hard on the pupils. One day he took a birch rod and he hammered Laughlan over the back of the neck and Laughlan went blind.

Well, then the next son was Walter, Watty. There were thirteen in that family and they had to get out working pretty young to make a go of it. When Uncle Watty was thirteen his mother knit him his underwear and his toque and mitts, socks, and she made him his jackets and pants out of woollen cloth woven in Ayrs Mills in Lachute, Quebec, from wool that came from their own sheep on the farm. Then his father made him his beefskin moccasins. Away he went to the shanty, the lumber camp, imagine, when he was thirteen years old. And when he was in his late twenties he was made foreman. Oh, I am proud to be named after that man!

Uncle Watty was foreman on the log drives eleven times and he said the terror of that whole trip was when they got their logs and timber into the St. Lawrence. At Lake St. Peter there was a terrific whirlpool and they had to watch for headwinds and everything else to avoid that place. If they got their logs in there they'd be in there all summer; there was no way of pulling them out.

Uncle Watty would go down, deliver the logs, get all the papers signed up and get on a boat and come back up to Montreal, get on another boat and get on the Ottawa River to Cote du Midi near Lachute, Quebec, and walk over to visit his father and mother and the rest of the family. Then he'd walk back into the bush again. He told me when they were carrying in their supplies in the fall he has carried two hundred pounds of pork in two big cotton bags strapped to his shoulders and sometimes he'd have to wade through mud up to his knees, with two hundred pounds on his back!

A lot of people talk about work now but think of those log drivers; they had to start as soon as the ice on the rivers broke up in the spring and it was still very cold at night. They'd get their logs rolling and through the night the logs would float along the shore and by the morning they'd be all frozen together. Those men had to get those peaveys — something like a canthook with a pick and a long spike at the end — to pry them apart and that was a dangerous job.

Well, after Uncle Watty gave up lumberjacking, he bought the Farmers' Hotel at Fallbrook. They say he made a lot of changes there; saw that the rules were obeyed, no nonsense. That was before 1878.

Well, there wasn't much of a way of washing clothes in the old days, no cisterns or anything like that, so in the spring they'd gather up all the blankets and everything and do a big washing. They'd take a big cooler down to get water out of Bolton Creek, then they had to heat the water over a fire and wash all those clothes over the scrubbing board. And they'd just put lines up among the trees to hang the clothes on.

So Watty's trousers were washed in one of the washings and hung on the line but when they went to get them in they were gone. And he knew exactly where they were! But he was a quiet man and he didn't say anything but he knew the customer that had them.

Two years later the pants walked into the hotel on a man's legs. Watty noticed them and he walked around for a while and hummed and whistled a little. Then he went into the house and came out with a vest over his arm. This man was sitting down beside William Gallagher and Uncle Watty sat down on the other side of him. He laid the vest down beside the pants and he said to Gallagher, "Would you say those two pieces of cloth correspond?" William said, "Yes, I'd say they were off the same web." "Well," Uncle Watty says, "Those pants were taken off the clothesline two years ago and," he says, "I knew where they were and I knew they'd turn up! Now, Mister So-and-so, you get up there on the floor and take off those pants and go home in your shirttail!" And he did, he did. Walked home a half a mile. No nonsense about it! Oh, there's a lot of stories have never been told; oh, should've been recorded years ago.

My great uncle Archie Graham was a very powerful man; he worked in the bush up north every winter and got two men's wages, hewing timber. He'd come down in the spring and he would go to the grist mill to get the grain ground. In those days they weighed everything by "stone," that's the old English method; they had a fourteen-pound weight, that was one stone, a twenty-eight-pound weight, two stone, and a fifty-six-pound weight; that was the one the balance was on. Oh, there was nothing very accurate, you know. And Uncle Archie could slip his finger into the ring on that fifty-six-pound weight and write his name on the wall, that's the kind of a man he was!

Oh, he was a very solid old lad; nobody changed what he thought! One time the minister came to his house when Archie was an old man, and they were having tea. And this minister was talking up pretty good, you know, to the old gentleman, and he said, "You know, Mr. Graham, that other time that I was here preaching you called me something and I never forgot it." "Oh," Archie said, "what was that?" "Well," the minister said, "You called me a drollion!" The old man thought for a while. "Well," he said, "I guess if I thought it then, I still think it!" He wasn't backing down any. You know what a "drollion" is? Droll, a droll one.

My father was quite a man. When he was ninety-four he'd walk to Bob Ashby's and back, nearly five miles the two ways. One day Dr. Blair came along just as Dad came out of Bob's and asked him if he'd like a ride. Father said, "No, I'm out for a walk," and he walked the two-and-a-half miles home. He celebrated his ninetieth birthday on the seventh of July and he mowed hay all day with a scythe, oh, a terrible hot day, and my mother and sister, Morna, followed him around trying to get him to stop. He'd say, "No, the hay's got to be cut!" Oh, such a man, such a man!

He used to be in the habit of getting up early in the morning and taking a tablespoon of Epsom salts and one morning he made a mistake and he got a big tablespoon of saltpetre instead. We always thought about the size of a bean of saltpetre was enough for anybody. He saw he'd made a mistake and he told Mother. So she telephoned Dr. Dwyer and he told her to mix up mustard and water and get him to drink that to make him vomit. They gave him about a pound of mustard and water and it had no effect at all. But for some years before that, at regular intervals, he had been taking these queer touts. He'd clap his hands, walk around and then for three or four days he'd be white as snow, white as snow. The strange part of it was his identical twin Alex lived in Preston, British Columbia, and when Mother had a letter from Auntie they knew Alex

had had this tout the very same time as Father had had his, the same kind of a spell. I often heard this about identical twins and it was proven in our family. Uncle Alex never got better from his but Father never had them again after that day. My father died at ninety-five at seven o'clock in the evening in 1950 and my mother died at ninety-one at seven o'clock in the evening in 1960, just ten years apart.

The Pioneer Life

Father and Mother had four of a family; Mabel was born in December, 1892; I was born the first of October, 1894 and I was called after my Uncle Watty Cameron; another sister, Morna, was born in September, 1896, and my brother Hugh was born on the first day of the century, January the first, 1900. We all went to school from that house up on the hill, the blacksmith's house; down one hill, around the corner and up another hill or two to the school. Oh, used to be great sledding there for kids.

In later years Morna taught school, taught for forty-one years and Mabel worked as a bookkeeper; she was

*Morna, Mabel, Walter and Hugh Cameron with
their parents in 1945*

twenty-nine years at the agricultural office in Perth and oh, precision! She wouldn't leave a letter *i* without a dot, the *t*'s had to be crossed just perfect, just like the people that learned their trades and professions in the old country.

Well, Hugh went through training for a druggist, only lived to be forty-seven but lived every day of it. And I stayed at home, didn't know any better, learned the blacksmithing as I grew up — and talk about memories! And changes...

We had our own mine back of here, too. From 1863 to 1873 there was an iron mine running back on the Sheridan's Rapids Road. I don't know who was running it but there was no transportation like there is today — no trains in Perth at that time, no railway — and they would have to draw that iron ore from about three miles back to Fallbrook, then ten miles to Perth. From Sheridan's Rapids to Perth, that's thirteen miles. Then they had to take it from there to Rideau Ferry, seven more miles, and pile it on the wharf there. And they'd load the boat when they got a boat load, you know. But, imagine, twenty miles for a team of horses to draw that load of iron ore; and they

used to have what they called "topping" up at the top of the hill here and another bunch over on Foley's Hill, extra, you know, to top the load. The horses were over the worst of it then. And then they'd take the full load from there to Rideau Ferry.

There wasn't much money in iron ore then but it was a good grade — one of the best grades — up there. Well, the transportation killed the whole thing. It ran for ten years and the people around here got work there in the mines, you know. But imagine with a wagon and a team driving twenty miles with a load like that!

They made iron ore paint, too. In mining iron ore, they would come across what they called "pockets of putty." That was pure red oxide, not much stone in it. They would gather that and I can show you in the shop the old grinder that they put it through and ground it up. They mixed it with buttermilk and painted the buildings; that old blacksmith shop was painted with it, iron ore and buttermilk paint. Oh, yes, the buildings all around here were painted with it. And anybody that ever painted an old cupboard or a rocking chair with that iron ore paint knows *you cannot get it out*! It wasn't really a paint, it was more like a dye — a dark red mineral colour.

You see in those days there were no cheese factories. Any milk they had, they churned it; no cheese or anything. And people would churn butter in the old dash churn and there'd be lots of buttermilk to make the paint.

Well, then, about 1878, William Lees, William Blair and Watty Cameron started a cheese factory here and the people were glad to have an outlet for their milk. Uncle Watty looked after the business end of it; went all around and made the deals to get the milk out. From what we call the Bathurst Line it was ten miles to Dalhousie. A team would draw that milk down every morning ten miles over that rough road to the cheese factory; have it there at seven or eight in the morning and they got eight dollars a ton for their milk. After driving it ten miles with horses, over hills and everything else! You know, in those days you could buy cheese for twelve or fifteen cents a pound. Oh, those old people had to work hard for a living! You know, we've been getting it too easy.

Doesn't it look like that to you? I think we're in for some changes!

And we're not the only generation that's had decisions to make; the people that left the old country to come to this land had a lot of decisions to make. And you know how they happened to come to Canada? They were weavers in Scotland, a lot of them, and when the wages there got down to about twenty-five cents a week they had to get out. An awful lot of people came from Ireland during the potato famine. But they always were used to hardship, always used to hardship.

Some of the settlers had money enough to pay their passage and they made arrangements with the transportation people to bring over twenty-five pounds of oatmeal and on the ship they lived on three meals of oatmeal a day. And when they got to Canada and got to Brockville they couldn't go any farther. A lot of them had to put in the winter there, living on oatmeal; no vegetables, nothing else, and they took the scurvy and a lot of them died.

Then in the springtime they started coming north, in oxcarts and everyway, through the swamps. Got to Smiths Falls and Perth and they kept branching off and going up to the back country. The people from the Highlands of Scotland went to the Highlands of Dalhousie and that way. Afraid of the low land.

There's a little place south west of Watson's Corners used to be called Fiddler's Hill. The story goes that the settlers, after hiking through the woods and over those rocks, became so weary and discouraged that they just all sat down and some of them broke into tears. A young lad, one of the bunch, took out his fiddle and played a few cheery tunes and this encouraged them enough that they went ahead. And they built a fine community up there.

And the English people too, the tenant farmers, had no land of their own in the old country, just paying back to the lord of the manor. They came over here. And look how those old people stuck by each other, building buildings and, oh, everything. They used what talent they had and they got along because they had to. Those old grub hoes that I have up there in the shop, the blacksmith made them and they were made to pound holes in the ground among the stumps to plant potatoes and corn, to survive on! And in every place when

they were putting up a log building, there were what they called corner men; in our community there were five. Each man took a corner and he dressed the logs to fit into those old dovetailed corners, hewed the logs and everything. Oh, we don't know we're living now and we send more to the dump than our great-grandparents raised their whole family on.

But they had fish and lots of venison and things like that. And they knew about herbs and learned about the plants from the Indians. But a lot of people died young; a lot of young mothers, you can see if you go through an old cemetery.

My father's uncle buried seven sons with smallpox. Seven sons! And John Ashley on the tenth line, I think he buried three children with scarlet fever or diphtheria, one of those contagious fevers, anyway. And nobody'd go near them, the fever spread so fast. So he'd make a box and take it down and bury a child in the graveyard and then when he'd get back there'd be another one ready to go. Imagine that! And then one day his wife was carrying water up from the lake and putting it into a tub to wash and while she was down getting a couple of pailfuls, a little boy

14

drowned in the tub. Oh, they were hard times!

But you take those men that walked behind the walking ploughs and the harrows in the early days; you hardly heard of them having high or low blood pressure or heart attacks. And people walked in the rain and thought nothing of it, or sat there in a buggy driving home in the pouring rain and be just dreeping! Oh, just another day! Just another day.

When they were taking sulphur and molasses in the spring, the old spring tonic, you know, they were not supposed to get their feet wet, but when my dad went out fishing with the nets in the spring he'd be right up to his chest in the icy water. Oh, it seemed nothing could kill that man!

A lot of those old trades have gone; the cooper, the old shoemaker; and weren't those old trades fascinating? Wasn't everything? Imagine, you'd go into a shop and the fellow would measure your feet and make a pair of boots. And they were all right, most of them! I have "lasts" for making boots here at the shop yet. Some people had to have their boots custom made; they'd have terrible bunions. Oh, they must have made a lot of misfits too. I've heard my father talking about people having ingrowing toenails and cutting a piece out of the boot. I guess those bunions were a beggar; you never got that running barefoot; that was from an ill-fitting boot.

And the Indians were great tradespeople; used to make these beautiful baskets. Some people said they used black ash to make the baskets; it was ash, anyway. In the warm weather in the summer they would put these pieces in warmish water to let them soak whatever length of time they needed then take them out and take big clubs and pound the logs. There was a little layer between each year's growth and this would break down. They'd take this off then take it to the river again, let it soak again until they got to the end of the white wood. White wood is the sapwood, the red wood in the middle is no good for baskets.

Those old coopers did beautiful work too; they would saw and chop the trees and make pork barrels at two dollars a barrel! To put a barrel together took a lot of time; trial and error, you know. You'd often have to do it over and over. They'd sometimes burn out an old oil barrel to take the oil out; they'd char it.

15

You've heard the old folks talk about a barrel of flour? Well, a lot of people never saw a barrel of flour, and I didn't either! But in the old days there were no bags or anything to hold the flour, to handle it, so the coopers would make barrels with wooden staves. They'd fill them up and each barrel held 196 pounds of flour. Later on they got bags they made, two bags of flour out of one barrel, ninety-eight pounds; that's the way it was shipped in the old days when my father was young.

And you know what they used to tie the bags with? Moosewood bark! Did you ever hear of it? Years ago there used to be little trees in the bush, oh, I've seen lots of them; I haven't seen any lately. They were a kind of yellowish grey; a soft-looking tree and I never saw one taller than two feet. Well, you could take a branch of it at the top and the bark would peel right down to the bottom, soft as leather and tough! They used that to tie the bags at the grist mill. I don't know where you'd go to find it now but I guess it just got cultivated out and binder twine came along to take its place. I read somewhere that it was called mouseweed but I think the moose ate it, and I guess that's where it got the name.

With no twine in those days, they'd twist straw and bind the sheaves; bands, they called them. My mother could make bands to tie the sheaves; the older people generally stayed on in the house and the younger ones would work outside. In those days there was nearly always a maiden aunt in the home. She'd look after the house — spinning and cooking. The wife would probably be out helping the husband with the grain. The wives worked out then, too, you know, but in a different way from today.

Empty barrels were very useful things; oh, they were used for dog houses, chicken coops, everything! Made hammocks out of the staves too. One old lad came in one day and asked, "Would you have an empty barrel of flour that I could take home and make a chicken coop for a couple of little pigs?"

The mills were important to a community. Alex Wallace was one of the pioneer millwrights, born and brought up in Scotland and served seven years as an apprentice. He went for a year, either to Glasgow or Edinburgh College, and took a course like an architect now. He was a special kind of millwright and he had wonderful instruments. A very serious man; they called him "the fiery little Scotchman." Everything had to go his way.

They used to say if you went to Alex Wallace and talked about a mill and took him to the place, he would look over the banks where you wanted to build the mill to know what water it would contain and the head you could get, the amount of water it could store back; and what they called the mill race; that was to let the water away when it went through the wheel. If it lodged there you wouldn't have the power. And he would measure it all up and take the leverage, ask a lot of questions; which side of the river you wanted the mill, where the logs were, and all the rest.

When he got all his questions answered and understood exactly what you wanted, even if it was four o'clock in the afternoon, he'd ask, "Where am I going to sleep tonight?" And he'd take off his clothes and go to bed. And he'd say: "You have so many men there at seven o'clock in the morning!" He was one of those men that had great leadership; he'd work hard himself and keep ten, twelve or fifteen men all working too.

A lot of men work hard themselves but can't lay it out for others.

Alex Wallace built the precision mills. Grist mills were mills that had to have a lot of elevators and it was very important to have the right slopes on them. That was one of Alex's specialties. Were you ever in an old grist mill where everything was ground, the different grades of wheat and everything, and kernelled? Alex would have all those elevators in perfect running order. He'd build the waterwheel and everything. Oh, a terrific man! Then he built a woollen mill at Fallbrook on the Bolton Creek. Fallbrook was once called Bolton Creek, you know, and there were four mills along it at one time. Now a cow could drink the bit of water that flows through it.

The mill was a long way up from the water and Alex built the waterwheel to run that. Years after when the mill was closed down, somebody bought the old waterwheel and took it out. He said it was just as good as one of the modern turbines, Alex was so far ahead with his skill. A small wheel did a lot of work the way he had it built. They ran the woollen mill until about 1896 or 1897 and it was sold to Christopher

17

Donaldson at the sawmill. It burned in 1902, all the oil from the wool.

Christopher Donaldson at the sawmill, he was a genius; *he was a genius*! He was another man that could work hard all day himself and keep twelve or fifteen men busy, and there's very few people can do that! And a great man to build houses, too, a good carpenter. One time, after he'd semiretired from the sawmill, some council hired him to clear some land and he had men there with teams drawing the timber out. He was the boss but the men said he'd chop about two and a half cords of wood a day, himself! Oh, a terrific man, a big rawboned man; an outstanding man in our community. What those people brought to this country!

Those old people got along! They had no money but one helped the other. A community then was like a union now; they just worked together. Now, if you haven't got a whole lot of money you can't get anything done, and a million people idle! I'll tell you a little story. It happened in 1847 up at the foot of Dalhousie Lake. Two young folks took a notion to get married and they had bought a poor place, poor buildings and a poor house. They got up early in the morning, walked into Lanark, got married and walked home again.

When they got home all the neighbours were there with a big dinner on the table. The whole gang got in and sat down at the table, and what happened but the floor gave way! They just carried the table and everything out and had their dinner out in the yard. Then, after dinner — there's always a leader, you know! — "You take the oxen ... you take the broad axe ..." and so on and so on. They took the old floor out and they danced on the new one that night! Now wasn't that a great wedding present for those people! And look at the community they were in!

Another time, Big Dunk McLenaghan walked out to MacDonald's Corners. They always called MacDonald's Corners The Hill. Every way you went to MacDonald's Corners, you went up a hill. From four sides! Dunk said, "Look, it's a good night, so-and-so has his leg broke and he'll be in bed for a while. Take your cradles," — grain cradles you know — "we're going to cut that field of grain; it's just ready to be cut. A good, clear moonlight night and it might be wet in the morning!"

And you know what they called

that? A fairy deed. That was the old Scotch way of doing business. A fairy deed! Cut the grain by the light of the harvest moon. Now you'd have to write to Toronto and have a head engineer come down and look the field over and so on and so on ... and in about two months you'd get permission to take off the grain.

William Lees did a lot for the community here. He started that grist mill and customers came from miles and miles in every direction. That was the first power the people had, the water power, and he had a grist mill, carding mill, shingle mill and sawmill. And he became member of the provincial parliament, too. Oh, he did a lot!

His father had been a miller in Oswego, New York, but he thought there was more future here and he and his wife came to Canada around 1820. But, oh, she was a social lady and Canada had nothing for her. She went to bed and sulked and stayed there the rest of her life, ran the business by remote control. Young William had no school to go to in Fallbrook and I guess he wanted an education, so he'd walk up on Sunday afternoons to Elphin, to Wilson's home. These Wilson people were, I think, the parents of that young man that was in the last duel in Canada, in Perth. Mr. Wilson had come out with a good education and William Lees would work on the farm and study at night by candlelight. That's the way he got his education.

That man Lees was quite a doer. In 1860 he bought 300 acres between lot ten and eleven, the east half of lot twenty and the whole of lot twenty-one. That took in the village of Fallbrook quite a way up. And when he got going — and his mills got going — people got work and then they started to build around there. By 1865 he had his mills going and he had to have a blacksmith. He built our shop and the back part of our house — Dad's house, up on the hill — the same year.

They say Dr. Bell, the Presbyterian minister in Perth in the old days, was going past a house one day and heard somebody playing a violin. And, oh, the old Presbyterians were terribly strict! He went to the door and he said, "D'ye not know the fourth commandment?" And the young lad said, "If you can whistle it, I can play it!"

19

2
A Victorian Boyhood

Earliest Memories

You know, people tell me they can't remember anything until they were about eight years old. Now, could that be, now, could that be? And there's people ask me the same questions, the same questions every two or three years. They can't remember ...

Well, sir, I've had quite a life ... and talk about memories! John Fumerton sold the store in Fallbrook to John L. Playfair in November 1896 and I was twenty-five months old. I can remember before they moved away, Mother took me over to the back fence — around the back of our blacksmith shop — and the two women were talking through the fence. I can see Mrs. Fumerton yet,

going and getting two handfuls of grapes from the vines growing there and putting them through the fence, one for my mother and one for me.

Fumerton had an auction sale and my sister Mabel took me to the sale with her. Well, Father was at the sale and when he saw us there he sent Mabel back home with me to get my face washed; I'd been around the blacksmith shop, you know. We got back again to the sale and there was a man up on the verandah and I thought I never heard anybody talking as much as that man ... and it was the auctioneer! Quite an experience for a young lad twenty-five-months old.

Father bought the bread box, the dough box with a lid, that day. We

The house where Walter grew up

came home with him and he held the gate open for us and I remember him carrying the bread box home up the hill and showing it to Mother. I can see it as plain as day! And she was pleased, I can remember that.

I've always lived near the Fall River. We owned that house up on the hill; the four of us were born there and went to school from there. The brick part was built in 1898 when I'd be about four years old; the back part, the wooden part, was built the same year as the blacksmith shop, in 1865. The old house wasn't log. William Lees had the early sawmill and he built the blacksmith shop and the house for the blacksmith in the

21

same year. It was built of two-inch planks, standing on end and dowelled together; they knew how to build, those old lads.

When I was four years old, Father got a notion he wanted to move that part of the house back and give it a quarter turn and in those days they didn't have much to work with. Well, they got the house up on skids and Johnny Bain brought up a stump puller he had; they got chains hitched onto trees and hitched onto the house someway and they manoeuvred around until they got that house where Father wanted it. And I can remember, as a little boy, standing with Mother in the house while it was moving. That was something wonderful and it was quite a feat for those men — no horses — with the equipment they had to move a house.

But before that Father had taken a notion to build a piece to the blacksmith shop; the front doors of the shop now face in a south-easterly direction but originally they faced the main road. So they went at it and they gave the old shop a quarter turn and built the woodworking shop onto it; that was in 1896. Oh, it seemed everything on that place had to have a quarter turn.

Oh, yes, I was around the old grist mill a lot. They had a kiln at the end of the mill where they dried the oats and corn and all that for oatmeal and rolled oats and cornmeal. People would bring in their own Indian corn and have it ground and they brought in their own buckwheat. They had an outfit there too that would hull the buckwheat and the oats and all and make buckwheat and oatmeal flour for the pancakes. And all those hulls went into the river. We could always tell when the men were hulling oats up at the mill: about seven in the morning we'd see the oat hulls come down the river — oh, just like bales of hay floating down. But now they make that into stock feed.

Pea brose, too — I saw them making pea brose; did you ever eat pea brose? There was a kiln up there at the end of the grist mill and it was about twenty feet square. The floor of it was tin and somebody had punched nail holes through the tin to let the heat come up. There was a big furnace below and the tin floor would get hot. They put the peas out on that and roasted them like peanuts, then they were ground up very, very fine, oh, just like dust; it had to go through a silk screen. I've seen the whole process. Pea brose was an old Scottish tradition. They'd put about three tablespoons in a porridge dish or bowl, put a chunk of butter in and a little salt and pour boiling water over it. Stir it up, and it was good, it was good! So fine, you know, the hot water would cook it, wouldn't take much to cook it. But very strong.

And I can taste that old stone-ground flour bread yet — wonderful! The loaves were not very high and they were dark but oh, it was good. Mother used to make a loaf in a pie plate for Sunday morning, a round loaf about so high and oh, that was wonderful!

Father bought two little cheeses every fall, one skim milk and one whole milk, and did we young lads ever like that skim milk cheese! In the old days there was a front door in the cookstove and a kind of a grate door in front of that and we'd open the front door and hold a forkful of cheese in there to get it warmed. It was just like rubber but did we ever enjoy that! Old Mrs. Rutherford on the Bathurst Line made it. Her great-grandson was telling me they have

part of the old cheese press yet, an old home-made press. It had a big lever and they'd put stones over for a press.

The carding mill closed in 1898. I can remember quite well seeing the buggies going past Father's house with bed sheets full of wool in the back. They'd have the sheet corners tied together with the sheep's wool inside, taking it up to the mill to get it carded, ready for spinning. Oh yes, and I remember my father taking me into that place — I don't know how old I was — but I thought I never heard as much noise in my life. Everything clicking and clacking, I wasn't used to it. There was a little wooden bridge with a railing on it. I can remember walking across that with my father, and this awful noise. And I can remember the two men working in the mill. And I remember the sawmill and the shingle mill. I worked in both of them when I was a lad.

I remember when the old woollen mill burned. The old building was just full of the oil out of the wool and it went up like a flash! Burned one day at about eleven o'clock when we were at school. I was about eight and oh, there was some excitement!

Christopher Donaldson had the sawmill at Fallbrook and he'd a great slide with a little carriage on it to bring the logs up out of the millpond. When we were kids we liked to watch that little car coming up with a load of logs. He rigged that all up. . . Oh, a wonderful man!

My mother and Mrs. Donaldson were great friends and one day Christopher came down in a terrible hurry, oh, just galloping. "Mrs. Cameron, come up, there's a baby coming! Come right away." "Well," she says, "I have some bread in the oven." "Oh, never mind the bread, never mind the bread, you have to come; we need you right away!" "Well," Mother said, "You go to the shop and tell Jim," — that was my father at the blacksmith shop — "to come up and take the bread out after a while and I'll be right up!"

Now that was neighbours! Mother was a midwife, everthing! She was a very smart woman and she had very good eyesight. I've seen her thread a needle in the moonlight. She was sitting sewing at the window and the moon was coming up. She'd a coal oil lamp on the sewing machine and something went wrong with the lamp. She sent my sister to the kitchen to get the lamp fixed up and I was sitting beside her. She said, "Walter, do you want to see me thread a needle in the moonlight?" And I said, "Yes, I do." And she put the thread through the eye of the needle with just the moon shining through the window. I guess that's where I get my good eyesight.

When I was a young lad, before we got the telephone in the village, if my father wanted a horse doctor, he hitched up the horse and drove into Perth and wakened up the veterinarian. Got him out of bed and he'd go out. And if you needed a doctor at the house, the same thing! I had kidney trouble when I was five years old. The doctor was brought out seventeen times and I saw the bill receipted. A dollar fifty a trip! It'd be twenty dollars now, for one trip.

My father used to pull his own teeth! Did you ever see a wax end? It's that hemp thread, about four-ply with sewing wax put on it; the kind you'd sew harness with. He'd measure it, make it just the right length, then he'd get us young lads to put a double loop on the tooth he wanted out. Then

24

A doctor's bill from 1900

plugged one time, filled, you know, and he always said he should never have got it plugged, he should've just pulled it out himself. Old Dr. Kennedy was the dentist in Perth then. I got teeth filled with him and the way he did it, he ground the hole with a thing like a knitting needle with a wee burl on the end of it and he kept turning that till he had it right for filling. Fifty cents! Imagine!

School Days

I started to school when I was five years old; I was six on the first of October. Went from April until June. There was just one room in the school and there were so many of us the seats were all filled up and there were benches around the wall. I sat on a bench holding my slate from April until June and I never got writing anything on it, the teacher was so busy.

I didn't do any sketching the first year at school, I was too scared. I went from April until June but I was afraid of everything, especially the teacher...

Teachers? Oh, I'd just as soon not talk about the teachers, I'd have to

he'd give that thread a good whack and that tooth'd just fly! Snap right out! He went to almost ninety-five and he spent fifty cents on his teeth in ninety-five years! He got one tooth

Walter Cameron, in his first year at school, is sixth from the left in the second row between sister

Mabel and Bill Ashby. Lloyd McKerracher is in front in a sailor suit

use some rough language.

That summer they built the second room onto the school and we all got going but we all used slates for quite a while. We had one teacher that was ... well, I've seen people that were more popular! At noon we could buy slate pencils down at McKerracher's store and one side of them was hard. There was paper twisted around them at a kind of an angle and we'd get all set to after dinner to work on our slates. We'd turn the squeaky side

and well sir, lookit, it would drive anybody up the wall! Oh, it was wild! But of course *we* wouldn't notice it. Oh, we had a good time at school, a good time, and the work didn't do us any harm! Two and two made four then, you know.

I could draw well when I was young and when it got near the time when our drawing books had to be handed in I got some wonderful apples out in the woodshed as pay for drawing in other people's books! And I was

26

forced to memorize miles of poetry for drawing pictures of the teacher. Maybe she thought she was better looking than the pictures. I can still remember some of the poetry. The poem "The Village Blacksmith" was in our reader and I couldn't wait to get learning that, and I still recite it.

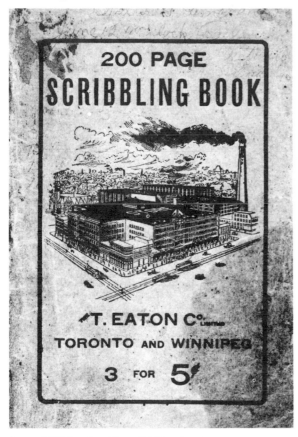

One of Walter's old scribbling books

The first toys I played with, I made them. In those days there weren't toys in the store and no money for things like that. I'd get some old bits of wood and make little buggies or wagons or hand sleighs and maybe put a bit of paint on them. Oh, I was making hand sleighs when I was seven or eight years old; I don't know when I started. It didn't do me any harm, didn't do me any harm! And, boys, when I was making a hand sleigh I was proud of it. Oh, we spent a lot of time sliding downhill in the winter.

Yes, most of the toys we made ourselves. The crooked breastbone of a goose made a good toy. You see, it was curved and heavier than in the other fowl; we bored holes at the ends of the prongs and put wax in the crotch of the bone and made a swifter — a twist like a spring. And we used to put a thread through a button too, and twist it. But that could be dangerous; one lad lost the sight of an eye with one of those. And, oh, I whittled tops! People kept bringing me the old wooden spools. If you cut a big wooden spool in two it would make two tops. Then you'd fit in a little piece of cedar or something in through the hole and out the bottom; the end would have to be pointed nice and smooth. Then you'd give it a good twirl and those things would spin! Oh, there was a knack to it.

We made bows and arrows too and slings for throwing stones, all hand made; we made the bows out of a bit of a willow. It was springy, you know. Oh, we never could hit anything, just played around. I can show you a little pair of tongs that I made before I was twelve years old. Oh, they have a few things wrong with them, but imagine, making them! Making the eyes, putting the rivet in; it's a great big rivet I put in. And I know it was before I was twelve because there was an old man that lived in the store then, used to be watching me making the tongs, and he moved away in 1908. And I'm proud of the darn things!

Stilts, kites, oh, yes, there was a season for everything. I tell you we were taught to make something out of nothing. Now they make nothing out of something!

My brother Hugh and I used to go fishing. He'd catch the fish and I wouldn't. We had an old boat and we'd change ends; he'd fish from one end and I'd fish from the other. He'd catch fish and I wouldn't. And we'd change fishing outfits too and he'd catch them and I wouldn't. So that sickened me of fishing!

We didn't go swimming much; the water in the Fall River past the house here was always too dirty, always full of sawdust and sticks and oat hulls from the mills up the river. Oh, everything was dumped in the river, but it was warmer than Bolton Creek. The river came down through the lake but Bolton Creek was spring fed and it was too cold for swimming.

How long is it since you've heard a boy whistle? When I was in school I was the official whistle maker. We made them in the spring when the sap was coming up in the basswood and I graduated in the whittling class by having three whistles on one piece of wood. I got a crotch of a basswood stem, Y-shaped, and made a whistle on each prong. That was the highest honour you could get in the whistle making. I always had a good jackknife, always had, and I kept it sharp.

Oh, I've had a busy life! The first job I got was a rough one. I was eight years old. It was looking after the

Mabel Cameron, seven years old, Morna, three, and Walter, five

school, two rooms in the school. I swept them and dusted them, carried in the wood in the cold weather, lit the fires at seven o'clock in the morning in the winter and shovelled the snow around the two entrances and around the two outhouses and everything. And how much do you think I got for it? Eight dollars a year.

There was no income tax then! Now, young lads have little or nothing to do, only just shovel a bit of snow. But I did *that* after school! I swept the two rooms, carried in the wood for the two stoves and then I went home and cleaned the stable for two cows and a horse and put down the hay, watered the horse and the two cows and then I fed the hens before dark. Then carried in the wood for the house and carried the water in. In the morning I had to go back to the school at seven and get working there. It didn't do me a bit of harm!

I think the thermometer went a lot lower years ago than it does now. Oh, the times my nose has been frozen, getting up to the school at seven o'clock in the morning, up the hill to put a fire in that school. Some mornings I could hardly get the key in the lock, my hands would be that stiff.

Oh, there were lots of chores to be done. The night before wash day we would carry water up from the river for Mother and put it in a big boiler. And in the winter time we'd go and get big icicles — there was a great place in the back of the blacksmith shop for icicles, oh, they'd be that size — we'd go and smash them up and put them in the big boiler at night and they'd be melted by the morning. And we'd carry in snow to melt. Oh, a lot of people don't remember the hardships!

When we were going to school we

William Lee's sawmill photographed in 1916. Wood fibre is pouring from the window. The young man in the boat is Hugh Cameron, Walter's brother

were always looking for work and Bruce Lees up at the sawmill always had lots of slab wood to pile. It was cut two feet long and we piled hundreds of cords. And one summer, when I was about twelve, something happened to the man who packed shingles so Bruce came down and asked if I could go up and pack shingles. "Oh," Mother said, "Walter couldn't lift a big pack of shingles." "Well," Bruce said, "if he'd come up and pack them, the men would take them out of the boxes and pile them up." So I did that for two or three summers — just a child, you know. Some days I'd pack thirteen to fourteen thousand, two cents a pack!

One Saturday morning when I was about fourteen years old, Bruce came

30

down and said they had a lumber culler there. The companies used to send in a man to cull the lumber as it came off the sawmill. It was two-inch hemlock plank and I went up that day and I handled thirty-two thousand hemlock pulp planks. I was taking a man's place but boys, oh, boys, I had an awful job getting out of bed in the morning!

When we were young, Dad wouldn't go to church but his Bible was well read. He was a great singer and every Sunday night he'd get the family singing all the old hymns, no music, you know. Mother used to send us to the little Methodist church back of Playfairville and when I got old enough to drive a horse we went to Balderson church; it was Presbyterian then, up until 1925, then it went United. But, imagine, just singing with no music; oh, Father had a good voice.

The gramophone caused quite a stir when it first came into the community. It had a big horn on it for the sound to come out and the dog's picture — a little white dog with black spots — and His Master's Voice in big letters; the dog was supposed to be listening. Oh, we couldn't believe that at all! Somebody was telling me that one old fellow got an old Victor gramophone — or somebody in his family did — and his wife said that this old fellow thought the devil was in it and he wanted to smash it with the axe. Oh, I guess they had a terrible time explaining it. It was unheard of, a voice coming out of a box, somebody roaring from California or someplace. If you never heard one before, it could be pretty serious! We had mostly hymns and Harry Lauder, records like that.

Lloyd McKerracher was the first boy in the school to have a pair of gum rubber boots; his parents had the store then. Oh, I remember the four eyelets in them and the leather laces; that was really something. Before that we all wore leather boots — beef hide — or moccasins, beefskin moccasins. They'd be made from oil-tanned leather so they'd pretty well be weatherproof. Lots of people wore moccasins; my grandfather had made them for his boys and Father made some for us. He had to make a little wooden form the shape of your foot first. Oh, people could *do* things in those days; they either made do or did without; no money.

31

We liked to think we were playing hockey. We'd get a little cedar tree out on the side hill, one with a crook on it; then clear off the branches, flatten the bottom, cut it just the right length and that'd be our hockey stick. Then, for a puck we'd find something frozen along the road, in the days when there were no cars. Worked just as good, just as good, and it wasn't expensive!

We'd have a Christmas tree at school and have a concert. I remember one time a girl got up to say a recitation about Christmas. I don't remember it all but every verse ended with, "For tomorrow is Christmas morning!" This old lad at the back of the room would always interrupt and shout, "It is not, it's the day after!" He was feeling pretty happy but the poor girl got so flustered she started repeating the verses. He'd interrupt her after every verse; they couldn't shut him up, I guess, so they finally took her off the stage. Oh, dear!

I remember the first time I had ice cream. There was a social up at the school and they borrowed a big freezer somewhere. They mixed up eggs and milk and stuff — a custard you know — and put it in the inside can. They packed salt and pieces of ice around the outside in the big wooden freezer bucket. The crank fitted through the lid and attached to a kind of paddle affair in the inside can. Well sir, we turned that crank and turned that crank and it would get harder to turn as the cream froze. When we couldn't turn it any more they took the lid off and gave us a saucer of ice cream, the first ice cream I ever got and I'd be ten or twelve then. Oh, I guess we earned our ice cream!

I guess I was about in the high school entrance class when I got my bicycle. Mine cost two dollars and I had to fix it up a lot. Oh, a new one cost around twenty-some dollars then, and this old teacher that wasn't too popular was coming up the school hill one morning with her satchel, her brown satchel, that she had all her books and lunch and everything in.

Johnny Bain had never been on a bicycle before but we got him up to the top of the hill and persuaded him it was no trouble to wheel down again. The teacher was coming up the hill. He hadn't gone very far till he couldn't keep his feet on the pedals and he just spread his legs like a frog. The teacher saw him coming and she took to one side of the road but he took to that side too. She went sailing across with her satchel and he hit her arm and knocked her and brown satchel end over end.

This teacher used to board down the road and one morning she had to go to the post office; the mail came at nine o'clock. So she put the satchel in some cedar bushes at the end of the bridge and when she got inside the post office the lads put a chipmunk they had caught into her satchel, just so it wouldn't get lost, you know! The teacher came out and grabbed up the satchel, walked up to the school and set it down. She opened the door and had the Lord's prayer, then she picked up the satchel and put it on her desk to get something out of it. And this darn chipmunk ran up her arm and over the back of her neck. Oh, she was in a bad humour about that! Some of the early men teachers — the old schoolmasters — were pretty rough. A lot of them were old soldiers, drunkards and everything.

Pranks and Mischief

Oh, I think it was a lot more fun in a country school than in a town school. There was an old couple who lived where the store is now. They didn't run the store but they owned it. The old lady used to scold us young lads terrible. Lloyd McKerracher and I were always together going to school. Everytime we'd go by she'd scold us for something! And sometimes little boys don't appreciate that!

One day the old couple was away and we had kind of talked it all over and we thought we'd go up to the grist mill and get some seeds. So we went up and told the miller what we were planning. He ran the grist mill and the fanning mill and he didn't get along with her too well, either. He said, "Lookit, boys, just fill your pockets full of seeds, corn and buckwheat and peas and everything, and go and plant them for her." So we went down and planted everything we could think of in her garden. A week or two later the seeds started coming up and when we walked past we'd hear her say, "I can't understand it. I put the sweet peas down here and

Lloyd McKerracher in 1818

lookit, they're coming up down there. I can't understand it at all." And the next week she'd say, grumbling away, "George says that's buckwheat but where could it come from, I planted flowers there?" And after a while the corn started coming up too.

Lloyd was an awful boy to laugh, oh, he'd just go into kinks. So I would keep asking her questions and Lloyd would be around the corner and I could just feel the ground shaking with his laughing. When I got all the information I said to Mother, "Come on down and see the beautiful garden Mrs. Campbell has." The two of us went down and the old lady, she started explaining all that was wrong with her garden. "Buckwheat there — George says it's buckwheat — and there's corn there, but how could the corn be coming up there?" And every little while Mother would take a queer look at me and say nothing. When she got through with her visit and we got back to the corner by the blacksmith shop I laughed and Mother said, "Were you in on it?" "Yes." Well, sir, did she ever laugh! Oh, that was great for her. My mother taught us to laugh, you know. Well, there was really nothing bad about it and I think the lady from the store learned something from it too. Oh, people — most people — had a better sense of humour then than they do now!

At the time an old couple was running the store. There was a little box stove in it and people used to sit around it and talk and tell stories. I always carried a wee package of red pepper in my pocket; it was nice to have and one night when they weren't looking I just put a good pinch of it in the wee hole for the lid lifter to fit in. After a while the old lads started to

Mabel and Morna Cameron with neighbour John Barclay

sneeze and they kept sneezing and sneezing, sometimes at the same time and sometimes one after the other. The man that owned the store, said, "Violet, bring out another stick for the stove; it's just getting chilly enough here!" So Violet brought out a stick of wood and when she stirred the lid lifter to put in the wood they got to sneezing all the worse! The hotter the stove, the better the pepper worked. The old fellow would

take his pipe out of his mouth and hold it away out to one side and go right to it, sneezing and sneezing.

The old lad that kept the store would start calling again, "Violet, would you bring out my old sweater? It's just chilly enough here!" So she brought out his old sweater and he put it on and kept sneezing and sneezing. After a while he shouted again, "Violet, bring out a safety pin to put in my collar." So she brought out a safety pin and buckled it right up tight, but they still sneezed and sneezed, oh, something terrible! Before he got through he had his old teamster's cap on down over his ears, sitting beside the stove! Oh, it was one of the funniest things I think I ever saw!

I was sorry about it afterwards.

Tollgates and Oxbells

I often think about the old tollgate in Fallbrook that was across the river from me. The bridge — the old bridge — was farther up the river and then the old road just cut right off across the bridge and around the hill. Well, the old tollgate ran until 1904 and I don't know if there's another person still living who has paid toll at that gate.

There were four tollgates and anybody going to Perth with a single horse had to pay five cents at each place. In those days that was a lot of money. Well, in the winter time they used to go in past Lee's grist mill and take the side roads and then go down onto the creek and go in on the ice. Oh, it was great going on the ice; they

had level road all the way along and they saved all those tolls! You couldn't blame them, a nickel was a nickel then.

I think the people who ran the tollgate got free rent for looking after it. The tollgate was attached to a house and I can still see that little tin dish they had for putting the money in. Well, in 1904 they changed the whole road system. They started putting stone on the road and they cut out the tollgates. You see, until then the tollgates had paid for the upkeep of the roads. After 1904 people had to pay for the road by taxes. They used to buy a lot of stone and pile it at different places along the road from Balderson to Perth. Frank Hunter would smash it up with this little hammer, oh, peck away at it all day; put it in the wheelbarrow and take it out and put it on the low spots. They called that a macadamized road.

I can remember oxen pretty well; there were two old brothers who lived up on the Heilan Line — the way the old Scottish people would say Highland, Heilan Line — and they would come down once every year with five or six long, cotton bags of

A Plairfairville community picnic in 1888. From left to right, James Cameron, neighbour Agnes Wallace, neighbours Foley and McMartin, Carrie Playfair, Annie Kerr, Mrs. Walter Cameron (Aunt Marjorie)

wheat to be ground at Lee's grist mill. They generally came along as we came out of school when we were going home for dinner.

We'd follow them and watch the old oxen and the great big wheels on the cart would be squawking and screeching just like a flock of wild geese. The old man walked ten or fifteen feet ahead of them with his staff. He wore an old-fashioned hat, a big high felt hat, a stovepipe hat with a wide brim. The oxen would follow him right along up to the grist mill. They'd unload the bags, turn around and put the oxen in the shed where the horses would be tied while they were waiting on the grist. When the grain was ground, they put everything in the oxcart again. I suppose it would be dark before they got home. A whole day's trip!

The old people said, when the oxen were going away from home they'd walk about two miles an hour. When they were going home, about two-and-a-half miles an hour — anxious to get home.

Years ago there was a family about a half a mile from Fallbrook; they had a lot of sons and the boys did most of the work. The father had either a good or a bad habit of sitting around the house a lot. One day the boys came up to the house with the team on the wagon and they had the wagon box on. The father went out and he was looking around and he said, "There it is again; you've got the front-end board where the back one should be, mixed them up again! Go into the house and bring out a piece of charcoal and I'll mark them so that you'll never get them mixed up again!" One of the lads went in and brought out a piece of charcoal. "Come around to the front here now and we'll put this B on here for Before," the old lad says, "and we'll put B on this board for Behind. Now never let me catch you getting them mixed up again!"

A tremendous lot of wood used to go through here on the way to Perth; everybody in town still used wood for heating their houses and for cooking and baking and I can remember the days when there'd be a row of sleigh-loads of wood that stretched half-a-mile and on both sides of the street! It came into Perth from the townships of Drummond, from Burgess, from around here and from the third line. One evening we stood on the bank up there at home and counted thirty-five teams and sleighs going empty past our place on their way home from Perth. That's in one bunch! Oh, there'd be an awful lot of wood waiting to be sold. And everybody happy! The old fellows standing around bantering, trying to sell it. And the sheds — there were four or five hotels in town then — and the sheds and the stables were full of horses. Everybody was talking horses and having a good time. And trading horses too.

One old fellow would be picking away at the wood all winter; if there was a knot in the wood he wouldn't buy it. And he went up to Archie Foster — Archie was a joker — and he said, "What kind of wood is that you've got?" and Archie says, "Wooden wood." "Oh," the old fellow said, "You think you're smart. Is there any other kind?" "Oh, yes," Archie said, "We've ironwood!"

Life is full of challenges; if there was ever a challenge in something, I wanted to do it! And if I wanted to do something badly enough, I could find a way. My father always used to say,

The village of Fallbrook with Walter's blacksmith shop in the foreground and the store, kept by his wife, next door

"Where there's a will, there's a way!" A lot of people say they can't. That's just an excuse; they just don't want to tackle something because they're afraid they'll fail or because they'd sooner watch the television. I never liked those two words "I can't." So you know what I did? I just took the T off and went through my life without it!

I spent a lot of time around the blacksmith shop, watching, listening to the old stories, asking questions. I hung around the shop in my bare feet until I started working there with my father; then the sparks from the fire in the forge got between my toes and I had to put on boots. But, you know, when people went in their bare feet you didn't hear about "hammer toe" and all those troubles!

3

A Blacksmith's Life

The Apprentice

I can't really say when I started blacksmithing; I've been at it since I was no size. But after a year of high school I started working with my father as an apprentice on the seventh of June, 1912.

When I was sixteen years of age there was not much choice of work. You either did horseshoeing or hard work! Looking back now I have no reason for regrets or apologies. There was not a night I couldn't say, "I did a man's work today." I had a good training from my father; he was a quiet man but when he talked he said something, and when he did something, he did a good job. He used to say, "If you're not going to do a good job, don't start it."

Oh, I've seen a lot of changes since I joined my father in the old shop. When I first started in the blacksmith trade we'd run to the door or window if we heard a motor car coming down the road; now I rush to the door if I hear a horse coming! But you know something? I'd rather be driving behind my little grey horse, Andy, yet! Oh, I dunno; we had a lot of good times with the old horses too. And I always had a great respect for a man who was good to his horses.

Going to town on a Saturday night we were into the racing, head over heels! But there were young men that didn't know a thing about a horse who would hire a good livery horse in Perth and drive it for twelve miles as

Walter Cameron at his forge

hard as it could go and go to Lanark and tie it in the shed, red hot. Go to a dance and that horse would freeze to death. I'm glad horses are out of it for that; oh, the same way they drove cars later. But cars have no feelings, cars have no feelings!

A fellow went to Perth to buy a horse one day and when this lad showed him a horse the man asked him: "Is it a good horse?" "Oh, yes, it's a good one! He can go to Lanark in fifty minutes and back in the same length of time!" And the fellow

41

looking for a horse asked, "And did he ever do it?" "Oh, yes!" "Well," he said, "I don't want him!" He knew the horse had been overdone.

John McLenaghan of MacDonald's Corners had just the handiest team you ever saw. He had a pair of Appaloosas and when he'd take one out of the stall the other would come out and get on the other side of the pole with nobody leading him. My little grey team, Andy and Clara, would do that too; lead the mare out to the pole and the horse would follow her out and get in his place. People would wait to see me hitching up that team. Oh, that little horse would do anything I told him. If I had him in Perth, driving him alone, I'd put the lines in the turret and take the halter and whatever buggy I threw that halter in, that horse was right around and into the shafts. I found that in training a horse, the best secret is to do the very same thing every time, every time.

The French-Canadian horses were pretty well out in my time but descendants of them were around and everybody liked them. But the French-Canadian horse couldn't go fast and he couldn't step high and he wasn't heavy enough for big machinery so he became obsolete. Very small but sturdy; oh, tough! And just one of the family! I've heard them saying that if they got stuck on a hill when drawing heavy loads, if a man got on each one of their backs, they'd take the load in. The extra weight would hold their feet on the ground! Oh, yes, just didn't have weight enough to stay on the ground. But that was the courage they had; they were very wiry for their size.

Fred Darou's old blue horse, that was another one! Fred had been wanting a third horse. He had a good team he worked himself but Mrs. Darou and the boys had nothing to come down to the village with. So they went into Perth one day, to Devlin's Horse Exchange, and Fred told Tom what he wanted. Well, the nearest thing to it was a kind of a blue roan, a low-set horse but he was tender on the front feet. Tom said he was a good horse except for that. "Well," Fred says, "I don't care about that because Walter can fix that." So he bought him and took him home. A couple of days after Fred brought him down to the shop. He was pretty sore on the front feet and I made him a set

Over a century's accumulation of artifacts and cobwebs lies on the windowsills of the Cameron blacksmith shop

of hand-made shoes with dropped soles. I took my time and fixed the horse up. And away he went home, just fine. Well, sir, every time Mrs. Darou or the boys would drive that horse past our shop, that blue roan would drive in, in spite of them; they said they couldn't hold him out. He'd pull right up to the blacksmith shop door. I'd go out and take the hammer; pick up one foot and hammer every nail pretty hard and pick up the other foot and do the same thing. And away he'd go happy again! Now, wasn't there something nice about that old horse?

When I was a young lad we had a Holstein cow and she was a great cow

but you couldn't keep her in any field; she liked other people's pastures better than her own. Nothing would stop her from jumping fences. Well, then somebody told him if he put a horseshoe on her front feet, or on one foot, she couldn't jump; a cow has cloven hoofs and before they can jump they have to spread out the hoof to get the use of their front feet. If you put the horseshoe on it would hold the split hoof together and she couldn't jump. So Father went to work and he made a horseshoe to fit and he nailed it on solid and by golly, the old cow stayed in the field.

But then she had some other qualities we didn't like: take her into the stable and she'd kick the stars out of the sky! We had to rope her hind legs together to get her milked. Dad was usually busy in the blacksmith shop and I had to learn how to do it when I was pretty small. You'd put the rope around her legs — above her hock joints, in a kind of a figure eight — and draw them up and then again just above the cloutch, that's just above the hoof, put another figure eight on there and snub her solid. Then Mother could milk her. Well, I got the roping job; I was small and when she kicked I could dodge her but bigger people couldn't, she'd nail them every time! Oh, such a cow! I guess that's where I got my fear of cows. I could never enjoy working around a bunch of cows.

Well, after a while Dad got tired of this; I guess he was afraid somebody was going to get hurt. She was going to calve about March and oh, he had her fitted up pretty good. She had an udder on her that would shame those cattle at the agricultural fairs. So he sold her to Johnny Noonan. He was always buying cattle and shipping to Montreal. This was in 1905 and he got forty-five dollars for that cow! In 1905! When word got around that he got so much for her, people would come in and ask if that was right. Oh, forty-five dollars at that time was good money. Terrific! But the only tears we shed were because he hadn't got rid of her long ago.

When I first started to shoe horses we charged, for a new shoe, twenty-five cents up to number sixes; took them off, two for a quarter — we called them "removes." Remove and replace, two for a quarter. Imagine! It'd take you half an hour to take the shoes off and fit them up and put them back on and finish them. You'd use your nails and coal and your time, for twenty-five cents! I'll bet the time was worth about five cents; nobody counted their time in those days.

We raised the price in 1912, on the fifteenth of November. We raised the price from twenty-five cents to thirty cents for a new shoe — and they called us highway robbers! There was nearly a civil war! There were two blacksmiths who wouldn't join us and people used to go to them, drive ten miles to save five cents. But you know, in the old days, there was quite a little strife among the blacksmiths — who could do the best work. Some were good at one thing and some

NOTICE

We the undersigned Blacksmiths of the district have arranged a new schedule for horseshoeing to take affect on and after the 15th day of Nov. 1912.

New Shoes No. 0, 1, 2 at 25c per shoe
New Shoes No. 3 & 4s at 30c per shoe
New Shoes No. 5 & up at 35c per shoe
Resetting Shoes No. 0,1,2 at 15c per shoe
Resetting Shoes No. 3 & up 20c per shoe
 and 75c per set of 4
Bar Shoe 50c per shoe
Resetting Bar Shoes 25c each

WM. HAW, Perth	A. BUCHANAN, Playfair
P. FURLONG, Perth	M. McINTYRE, Elphin
J. H. McMILLAN, Perth	J. WILSON, McDonald's Corners
M. P. WHITE, Perth	S. McILRAITH, Lanark
J. ALLAN, Scotch Line	N. AFFLECK, Lanark
WM. DeWITT, Eliott	J. GALLINGER, Lanark
JAMES CONLON, Glen Tay	A. CRAIG, Middleville
WM. NOONAN, Balderson	R. SOMERVILLE, Middleville
A. SHEPPARD, Ferguson's Falls	T. MOLYNEAUX, Hopetown
BRUCE EDWARDS, Drummond Centre	J. LABELLE, Watson's Corners
A. LEIGHTON, Harper	W. J. WRATHALL, Poland
J. L. CAMERON, Fallbrook	E. J. McFARLANE, Lavant

This notice caused a stir when it was first posted in 1912

were good at something else.

Those macadamized roads were awful hard on the horses' feet. They just crushed the rock and put it down with little sharp corners on it. Some of the old drivers that were tender on the heels and had thin soles, they couldn't take it. I used to make round shoes, perfectly round, and that protected the heel; the horse could trot right along. And it was nice to do that for the horse and it was nice to do it for the owner; nobody liked to drive a lame horse. No foot, no horse!

Billy Lee had a little horse he liked very well, old Teddy, and he had very tender soles on his feet and weak heels. But I could shoe him so that he'd just go fine. One day, Bill was in town and he took him into the shop there; it was going to save him a half day. So they shod him in town and Bill and Teddy could hardly get home; he drove him along on the grass all the way home. And early the next morning Bill brought Teddy along what was called Anderson's sideroad, on the grass, all the way to my shop. Bill was just sweating about Teddy; he was ruined, he was just ruined! "Oh," I said, "We'll try him, Bill." So I just did it my way, put the shoes on and sprung the heel a little and made old Teddy comfortable. And the next time Bill was by he said, "What in blazes did you do?" "Well," I said, "Bill, I think they use bigger nails in town."

I always liked working with horses, and I was awful proud of our little grey horse Andy. He and I used to be out a lot together. We were young together. One time we were getting some rock elm cut up at Anderson's

Morna, Mabel and Hugh Cameron with Andy in 1918

Mill and Dad wanted to go up to give directions. So we hitched up this horse. I used to trade buggies when I was young and then I had an old buggy with no sides on the seat. We went up and got the load on at the mill and came out onto the road.

I said to Dad, "Did you ever see this horse trot?" I don't remember now what he said but the horse was just waiting to be let go. We came down that half mile at a fast trot and when we came to a little curve going

46

downhill, there was Johnny Ashby with his team with a load of manure, resting his horses in the middle of the road. And we didn't have four-wheeled brakes on in those days! We had to go somewhere! So we took the ditch.

When Dad saw this coming he had dropped down into the bottom of the buggy. We went round the corner of the garage, around the corner of the shop. And after we stopped at the stable door Dad climbed up out of the bottom of the buggy. When he got on his feet he hit his fist three or four times on the back wheel of the buggy and shouted, "Now, that'll do!" And away to the shop. Oh, the wildest ride he ever got!

Oh, everybody was proud of their horses. The old people that brought their horses to the shop, they just talked about Maude and Tom and all, just like one of the family. Some people had pretty good horses. I once overheard two old fellows talking: "You know Geordie Fallah? When he first came out to Fallbrook from Perth, he came out in an hour and five minutes!" "That's nothing," the other lad said, "Our Freddie came out with our horse in ninety-five minutes

and no hour about it!" There was a hundred minutes in his hour!

About sixty years ago Dad made a wheelbarrow for the cheese box factory up there for wheeling in the wood. Well, the young fellows thought this wheelbarrow was quite a novelty. He made it without sides on it, just to pile the wood on. One day some of them were going in to Lanark and the lads sent in for a bottle of "cough medicine" or something they used to sell at Dobie's Hotel. They got to tasting it, and tasting it, and by evening they were feeling pretty good and they started fooling around with this wheelbarrow. It was just about half moonlight. George Richardson — he was the miller's son — he got the wheelbarrow up on the railing of the bridge and he got cheesemaker Dave sitting in it. And he wheeled him across on that railing in the half moonlight with a little jog in the railing about every eight feet! They got there all right, but imagine, on the railing! And you hear about the drop at Niagara Falls!

But most of our time was spent at the blacksmith shop or out shoeing horses. When they were building a dam in 1918 at the High Falls — that was up at MacDonald's Corners — for the big electric station, some of the teams from around our area worked up there. They were getting six dollars a day and that was big wages in 1918.

In the fall of the year they had to start shoeing the horses so they came down to the village. And the day they came down with their horses to get shod and went back again, it meant they lost six dollars. And they were paying me six dollars for shoeing. So a bunch of them got together and they said, "Come up at night and we'll give you a dollar a shoe." A dollar a shoe seemed like a million dollars! I'd hitch up my little grey team after shoeing horses all day and I'd drive over those frozen roads, put my horses in the stable somewhere and back to the shoeing! I'd put on thirty-two shoes on those big horses, then hitch up and drive home, put the little grey team in the stable, get my breakfast and back then to shoeing horses till bedtime and never think a thing about it, just a day's work. They gave me a dollar a shoe, thirty-two dollars! I thought I'd never see another poor day!

That same year a good friend of mine came down to the shop. He used to live on the Gilchrist farm, east of the village, and he wanted me to go up and shoe a big heavy Percheron with a quarter crack, the hoof had split. "Oh, Jim," I said, "I couldn't go eighteen miles just to shoe one horse!" "Well," he said, "if you had more?" "Yes." "How many more?" "Oh," I said, I'd want quite a few." "Well," he said, "I have the grey team, a chestnut team, the brown team and a Clydesdale stallion. How would that do?" "Well," I said, "that's a good start, anyway."

So I went up there and he had an old bellows in the pig pen and an anvil and we worked for about an hour, plugging old pieces of rope into the cracks of the bellows just to hold air. Then we went at the horses and had three teams shod at noon. And then we shod the stallion. "Well, have you enough yet?" "No." Well, he phoned Peter White at Clarendon and Peter brought down the four-year-olds and we shod them. "Have you enough?" "No." So he got Billy Geddes to bring down a little light team he drove a lot and we put eight shoes on them. That made forty-four shoes!

On the wall in the blacksmith's shop

But oh, there was a picnic going on all the time! Bill Warrington was one of these real horse dealers. Bill had a different horse nearly every other day. So Bill was in this gang of horse traders and he had been in Lanark one day with a horse that he really wanted to get rid of. He met a man from a long way away and Bill thought he wouldn't see him again so they traded. But that next fall Bill and this man met again in Lanark and as soon as the lad saw Bill he knew him. "You're the man I traded horses with last spring!" "No! Nope! I guess it was my brother, Jim!" "No! It wasn't your brother Jim; it was you! What kind of a horse was that you gave me anyway?" "Why? What seems to be wrong with him?" "Well, it took three of us every morning to lift him up on his feet!" Bill said, "Well, I don't understand that; two of us could lift him a-a-ny morning when I had him!" Dear oh, dear!

A lot of the old blacksmiths traded horses on the side. There was one fellow at Jasper got one awful bad kicker. Sometimes those sharks would dope a horse so that he wouldn't kick and you could walk around him fine as long as the dope worked but as soon as it wore off he'd kick the stars out of the sky.

So the blacksmith got one of those but what could he do with it? Well, by golly, he sold it to a man and when it got home it just kicked the stall to pieces and the man brought it back. The blacksmith wouldn't take it back and the man wouldn't give him his money. So they went to court. The magistrate asked the blacksmith a lot of questions then he said, "Did you not tell this man that horse was a kicker?" And the blacksmith said, "No, I didn't. The man I got it from didn't tell me and I thought it was a secret."

Oh, there was something going on all the time. People gathered in the blacksmith shop. That's where we ran the government! We used to get the old fellas going; we knew the strong points and the weak points in most of the people and we tried to bring them out. Around election time was good. One old fellow would get so worked up he'd fire off his hat and throw it on the floor and jump on it.

We had our own way of making fun. I used to cut a lot of hair, people's hair. They didn't go to barbers much in those days. I'd get them sitting up on the old anvil and put a coal bag around their necks for sanitary reasons. Do you mind the clippers they had for horses' fetlocks? Well, I'd get them well oiled up and get them running pretty good. Some of them wanted their hair cut, oh, clipped right off clean! There was an old fellow used to come regular, twice a year, before he planted the potatoes in the spring and again before he dug them in the fall. Clip it right off short. So I got the clippers going pretty good and he was sitting on the anvil with a coal bag around his neck.

I said, "Now, hang on!" and he got hold of the bench and I started in with the clippers. We got up to that

50

little burly place up there and I started to back the clippers out and they cut a little. He said, "What's the matter?" "Oh," I said, "I just run into a nail." He put his hand up to feel where the nail was! I pulled teeth, too! Oh, take a blacksmith, they'd lots to do, a lot to do. . .

The Village Smithy

Oh, I did love the smell of the blacksmith shop, the horses standing around waiting to be shod, and the smell of the fire. I often wished I could've bottled the smell of the old shop just to keep. Oh, times have changed, going too fast for me.

When the old blacksmith shop was going strong everybody needed everybody! Now nobody needs anybody! Back in those days the farmers needed the blacksmith and the blacksmith needed the farmers! We were just like a big organization. We shod their horses, repaired their machinery — the machinery was all pulled by horses — and worked against time! Oh, we'd do a lot of their work at night; repairs you know, and they appreciated that.

Walter Cameron at the anvil he has used since 1912

One time they started what they called a syndicate. They had a threshing outfit and a corn cutter up around Watson's Corners. A whole lot of farmers owned it. Joe Mell and Jimmy Hart were running it that fall

51

and they broke a steel link that used to run on the cog wheels. And everybody wanted to corn cut as soon as they could possibly get it done. So they came to me with it and I couldn't repair it. And Joe Mell said, "What in the world are we going to do? Everybody's dying to get their corn cut." And I said, "Joe, I'll make you one." So I took a piece of band iron and cut it the right length, cut the centre out of it and curved it both ways and I made a perfect link. And a while after they came back down again to have something done and they told me they couldn't find which link I had made, it was so near the shape of the others. Oh, those threshing mills and corn cutters, they had to be kept going. That corn had to be cut at a certain time and the farmers depended on the blacksmith to get the work done. I had that reputation; find a way or make it. And I'm proud of that.

Billy Bedore was a welder from Ardoch, forty-eight miles from where I live. He came down one day and he told me he'd like me to weld a new end on a big well-drilling bar about, oh, seventeen feet long. It weighed 690 pounds. And, "Oh," I said, "my anvil's too small!" and I tried to put him off — a big job. And by golly, I looked out one day and there was Billy with an anvil it would take fourteen men to lift and the big bar! So! I was sunk crazy! My Dad said, "You could never do it; you'd be crazy to try!" But I didn't want to send him back forty-eight miles so I said, "Leave it, Bill." And we did a perfect job! Oh, a challenge you know, I do like a challenge!

There was a little mare that they took to a blacksmith's shop at Perth to be shod. Mick White was the shoer there. She got a-kicking and there was a nail drove through her shoe and it caught Mick in the neck. They put eleven stitches in his neck. Oh, you could see the jugular, just jumping in and out. The blacksmith yelled, "Get her out of here. Don't ever bring her back here again!"

But the man who owned her had to have her shod. His cousin was married to my wife's cousin and they were visiting one day. Our cousin said, "I'll bet Walter Cameron could shoe that mare. I'll go back with you and we'll see what he can do." The mare was a monomaniac, an old monomaniac. Her father was a mean old devil; they used to have to drive him with a kicking strap on him to stop him and that streak was in her, too. So they told me all about it; they were honest, didn't hold anything back. I said, "All right, I'd like to try it." So we got her in the shop and I said, "Lookit, if you can hold her head up high enough I can hold her foot; I don't care what she does." So we got the halter shank over a ring and held her head up. A horse can't kick worth a darn if its head's high up. We just kept her head up good and high. And I shod her, shod her for years. They'd drive from Perth where there were five or six blacksmiths, out to Fallbrook.

One of my secrets in shoeing a horse was to hold the foot where the horse was comfortable. A lot of people would hold the foot at an angle that upset the horse. And you could feel that in the horse. A lot of blacksmiths thought that if they kept away from a horse they were safer. But I kept in close. I'd rather get a kick close than from a distance, they can't kick you near as bad. And they're more comfortable! Oh, I've shod horses you couldn't tie at all — just left them loose and shod them. Oh, I tell you, if

people heard about some bad team coming there'd be quite a crowd gather around to watch. And a lot of the secret is, if you've nerve enough just to give a good roar and grab the foot and let him know you're going to put on that shoe whether he likes it or not, that lets him know who's boss. And it does him good.

I've shod horses that the owners wouldn't hold by the head; got somebody else to hold them. And I shod nearly all the colts — the first shoeing — in that country because they knew I'd take my time. That first shoeing is very important, you know. And a lot of people don't know that old secret. In harnessing or shoeing or anything the first time, a very good method is to give him about one-half of his own way, about half. And the next time half of that again. He's yours after that. Don't hold him down too tight but don't let him go. My father was an awful determined man; he'd stand out in the middle of the floor and they'd just chuck and jump all over the place and he'd go with them. But I'd get them up against the wall; got them shod far faster that way.

There's no two horses' feet the

same; no two people's feet the same! And I could get along with horses that other blacksmiths couldn't. I'd let them fight themselves or I outwitted them and I found there's some people horses like and there's some people horses do not like! Just like dogs. Some blacksmiths used to put twitches on them — that's a little rope on the upper lip to distract them — but I never did. A lot of the bad horses came from out West. And you know what made a Western horse hard to shoe? They'd been lassoed and thrown around and branded and they'd smelled that burned flesh. The next time they smelled that, it'd be at the blacksmith shop — burned hooves. Shoeing wouldn't hurt them but the smell, it just put them crazy, put them crazy!

I never liked shoeing horses in their own stable. But if a horse was brought out into the shop, his mind was taken up by other things and he was not as hard to shoe.

Horsehide is the best for a blacksmith's apron; sheepskin wouldn't last, shrinks when wet; deerskin's no good either. The old blacksmiths found that horsehide lasted longest. You see, horsehide is waterproof and the horses often come in to be shod with wet feet, oh, just dreeping wet. This apron I got is forty or fifty years old and I shod the horse it came off and his father and mother and grandfather.

I shod a lot of horses, a lot of horses. Big Jim MacLean used to come from Rideau Ferry with a big Western team and I'll tell you they were tough! The nigh horse, he had him in a blacksmith's shop in Perth and they fought him all afternoon and they couldn't get him shod; they'd ropes and everything and he was skinned all over. Jim says, "Never again will I get that horse roped." Well, my neighbour was a great booster of me and my work. He was working there with a team and MacLean was telling him all about it. And my neighbour said, "You take him to Walter Cameron and he'll shoe him just the same as any horse." And so one day about four o'clock he came along. He'd driven from Rideau Ferry where they were working on the road, seventeen miles. He told me all about them and I said, "I'd like to try it."

Two men were working with me then, oh, big fellows. Bob MacFarlane and I were going to Old Home Week

54

in Carleton Place that night; this was in 1924. And, by golly, we shod that team before six o'clock! When Jim went back he said "Cameron shod that team. He must have doped them but I never saw him do it! Never saw him do it." He drove down here for years from Rideau Ferry with the team in a wagon. Oh, I had a lot of fun.

Well, that night we all went down to Carleton Place. We had an old Model T Ford and oh, we parked somewhere. I don't know where and I don't know if we bothered to take the key out of it or not. We got wandering around and these two lads that had worked with me were pretty husky men and they found this place to test your strength. I think all along before that they'd been wondering who was who. So one of them got on this outfit and lifted 700 pounds and the other lifted 800. Then they wanted me to try it. I pretended I didn't understand how it worked so I fooled around and fooled around, then I tried it and by golly, I lifted 1,100 pounds! Oh, blacksmiths became muscular. They say that blacksmiths never could wear a belt, they became so full of muscles from their work.

Experience is quite a teacher, isn't it? I tell you, if you got a reputation for shoeing the bad ones, they'd bring all the rubbish in the country to you. I don't know whether it was because I didn't know any better, but I did it. I've never abused a horse — I've outwitted them. I found out how they fought all the other blacksmiths, then I'd try another way. Then the horse had to learn something. In the other case, he had it learned, how to beat the smith.

Bob Rutherford had a big heavy horse, twenty-one hundred and fifty or sixty pounds. Big Tom, they called him. And mind you, twenty-one hundred is a big, heavy horse. Bob came out one morning to the shop and wanted to have two shoes made for the other horse, Prince. He said, "Lookit, I've gotta draw these horses tonight at Lombardy. Could you come in and tack them on?" "Oh," I said, "All right." So I got in there and I finished them up, carried my tools out and put them in the truck, and I saw this Big Tom, and I just wondered.

Bob came out and he said, "Lookit, this fellow's a little pigheaded. Would you attempt to shoe him?" I said, "I'll try him, I'll try him." "Well," he said, "we've had several circuses with him, trying to get shoes on him. I had the vet out and he told me he put enough dope into that horse to put any three horses to sleep and it had no effect on Tom at all." He said they had put ropes on him, got him down, and after a while Tom took a notion to get up. And he just broke the ropes and got up. Oh, they had had a terrible time with him. Somehow word got about that maybe I could put that shoe on him and a whole lot of people gathered around, oh, a lot of people. One fellow took hold of Tom and in a split second he was upside down in the hay stall. He closed his eyes for a while, got up again, tried again. And the same thing happened. I said, "I never saw a horse do it that way — pure lightning."

So I picked up a shoe and the rasp. I set the shoe on a little bench. I had a block there. I went in and lifted up Tom's foot and I hammered four nails in. Just while he was thinking about it. I just put the foot down and pretended I was all winded, then I went and picked it up again and hammered four more nails in. Then, in a little while I clinched the nails, picked up my tools and went out and put them in the truck. Bob says "Here's five dollars for putting that shoe on." "Oh," I says, "Bob, I couldn't take five dollars for putting one shoe on a horse; give me a dollar." So he gave me a dollar and we were all happy; all happy!

Everybody was standing there with their mouths open, wondering what happened. So Bob said, "Lookit, will you tell me how you could take hold of that horse and put that shoe on him and he never minded it a bit? We've used ropes and everything else." I said, "Bob, I'm going to tell you this little secret and don't you tell anybody. I've known it for a long time; it's a very bad horse that will kick either a drunk man or a fool — and I never was drunk!"

Oh, I've got along well with bad horses. And the reason why I can carve horses with eyes that will follow you is that I've studied them and I got to know what each horse was thinking. I had that out of them whether it was worth the money for shoeing them or not. I dream about them yet but in my dreams I never can get a horse shod; there's always something goes wrong. I dream about those tough horses, oh, I've shod a lot of tough ones. And it didn't do me any harm; I didn't know enough to be afraid of them. Never was afraid of a horse but I would never go up among a bunch of cows for a million dollars a minute.

My father and I, between the two of us, we've had this blacksmith shop since 1888, that's ninety-one years, and I've been blacksmithing for sixty-seven years. The old shop's not going so speedy now but it's still going. Oh, I want to keep on! We had the woodworking shop attached to it too. I have an old chair here that was marked out with a scribe before lead pencils were used much. Father used to call the scribe the scratch-all. Hard working people; spent their lives in their own little community. Father said Queen Victoria was dead seven days before Fallbrook knew it. That was in 1901.

Yes, it was a busy spot, the blacksmith shop and woodworking shop and we were busiest in a dry summer. A lot of people dreaded a dry summer; there was no hay and things were pretty tough; the price of cattle would be away down. But a blacksmith always benefited by a dry summer; everybody's wagon tires or

A blacksmith's bill from 1902. Fallbrook was often spelled with a final E in those days

buggy tires would get loose in dry weather and the wood would shrink so the tires would have to be set. A blacksmith had a harvest in a dry year!

One time I went into Lanark to get Ed McFarlane, a retired blacksmith, to come out and help set tires. I had about sixty-eight wheels waiting and I needed help. Fifty cents a tire. Oh, and the work in it and the time and then paying a man out of that. We had to heat the tire, cut it, weld it and make it shorter. We'd put it on the wheel and all for fifty cents. Imagine, two or three hours' work for fifty cents. That shows the change in our business.

The blacksmiths that were here before my father used to make their own charcoal, right out here at the back of the shop. They'd have a pit, burn some kind of hardwood, keep it smouldering. They'd know just when to toss a bit of earth over it to keep it smouldering until the wood became charred. They'd watch it day and night.

Blacksmiths lived to be old, old men. My father was one of eight brothers, all powerful men, and my dad and his brother, Will, both blacksmiths, outlived them all. Worked hard and slept at night! Mother used to say there was something in the coal dust that made them live so long.

Father used to make his own horseshoe nails from the blades of the old Swedish scythes. They used to make the nails one at a time, the only way they had of making them. Oh, there have been a lot of changes and there's history in this old shop.

The James brothers in Perth had a big business away back and we got all our iron from them. Oh, we bought thousands of dollars' worth of material from George James at the foundry. I bought horseshoes, horseshoe nails, wagon rims, buggy rims, sleigh shoeing, thousands and thousands of bolts and thousands of plough points from their store. We used to get that bar iron for four cents a pound in Perth and the last I got in Ottawa was a dollar a pound. At one time James brothers owned the biggest hardware business in eastern Ontario. And a big machine shop, and two garages, and the foundry, and the rink. Ran them all!

George used to come out to our place almost every week and he'd bring out some retired man that had no way of travelling, just for the trip. And we'd have to go over to the shop and he'd find out what I was making and if I didn't sell him something he'd have to sell me something or the evening was spoiled. We had to do business one way or another. George came every August and said, "How are you going to be fixed for horseshoes this winter?" "Oh, I guess I'll need some." "Will you need a ton again?" "Oh, yes." Now that's twenty kegs of horseshoes. And I'd ask

"What's the price this year?" So he'd get out the book and start figuring. "Well," he'd say "if you pay in cash we'll have them brought in from the rolling mills in Montreal and you pick them up at the station; we won't need to lift them or do a thing." And we'd start figuring.

There used to be some great calendars put out. I've got calendars from the Capewell Horseshoe Nail Company, 1896, 1897 and 1898. We were among the biggest customers in eastern Ontario. Every three months the salesman would call around; if we could take ten, twenty-five-pound boxes of Capewell Horseshoe Nails, he'd throw in an extra twenty-five pounds, a bonus. Then we would take that 275 pounds of nails and we'd have to buy another assortment to run that bunch out.

At this time we were driving over one hundred pounds of horseshoe nails a month. And that took a lot of that stuff they used to call sweat. We used to say it took two men in the busy season carrying drinking water to us.

Then I would take that ton of horseshoes and at night, after the horses were away, I'd work till bedtime caulking up shoes for the winter. That's putting on metal studs to grip the ice. We called them corks. I caulked up a ton of horseshoe shafts, that's a lot of work. I worked about sixteen, seventeen hours a day. Then I'd have other work to do, too. Oh, in my time blacksmithing was a big job, a big, big job. No thought of cars or anything else taking over. They thought that horses and wagons and buggies would go on forever and ever.

I don't know of any job that I could've worked at where I could have done as much for the community as I did: shoeing their horses, repairing their ploughs and harrows, sleighs and buggies and everything else. Barbering and pulling teeth; doctoring too. Oh, a blacksmith was called upon to do a lot of jobs in those days, a lot of jobs!

4

Stories of Village Life

Horse Sense and Common Cures

Blacksmiths had a great experience, didn't they? They were asked to do a lot of different jobs and in some ways they were a real authority in the community.

You remember the old tubs for cooling the horseshoes? Just a half barrel, pretty well filled up with water. People used to come into the blacksmith shop and get bottles full of that to put on cows' teats, they said for "pock." Did you ever hear of that? It was little bumps. They'd fill up bottles and take it home to wash the cows' udders with it. What was in it I don't know but scales off the iron would settle in the bottom and then, when you'd empty out that tub,

there'd be three or four inches of thick sludge in the bottom. Whether that had anything to do with it I don't know.

Jack Anderson — we called him Big Jack — lived a mile down the river. You had to drive through four farms to get to his place and he had to open four gates when he came out in the summertime. Well, one time in the winter he came out with a horse and cutter to my father in a great splutter; had a cow choking with a small turnip in her neck. So Dad put on his coat and away he went. And as Dad was getting out of the cutter, he just took the buggy whip with him. Jack held the cow's head up, Dad took the butt of the whip and just pushed the turnip down the cow's neck and

Hugh and Walter Cameron

into her stomach and it was all over. Oh, just nerve, you know!

You see, they had to drive ten miles to get the vet and a lot could happen in that time. The old people just had to find a way to do it themselves and some of the old vets had to, too. Just like the blacksmiths. I was mighty lucky; well, not lucky in a way, but there was a veterinarian in Carleton Place who passed on. And a whole bunch of his horse doctoring books were put up for sale in a secondhand store, six or eight of them, and I saw them there. Oh, they were good books, the best for the time, and I bought them all up and took them home. Did I ever learn a lot about horses' feet and legs! I studied those books and that gave me quite a help in special shoeing.

That was just an opportunity and I took it. I found out all my life that when something knocks on your door, that's the time. You know the old-fashioned saying: "You never get a second chance to make a good first impression on anybody!" Now, isn't that true?

We would bleed horses and that seemed to cure nearly all the diseases they had in those days. Some people thought it was a terrible thing but that was a great cure at one time. Oh, I bled a lot of horses; the first one I bled I was sixteen years old. Horses used to take what they called farcy — that big swelled leg — and maybe a big lump along the belly. Bad blood, that's what they called it. I'd take a set of flames, they were three blades, like lances, the big one was easiest to hold. Dad made his own but I got a set in a little case like a jack-knife. I'd put a rope around the horse's neck down near the collar line till you could see the vein swelling. Just give the blade a little tap, take eight quarts, then take a pin, just a common pin. Put it through crossways, take a few hairs out of the mane and wind them around it. And that was it.

And for kidney infections, in people, when they couldn't pass water, they mixed up some kind of medicine from that cranesbill — a kind of wild geranium. Oh, those old people, they learned a lot, knew a lot of old cures. The old people tried things like that. They just had to. One helped the other and they'd pass on the remedies. I tell you I just worship some of those old people, what they did. Terrific! And they weren't given credit!

Morley Ashley's grandfather, Bill, and my father were great friends and Bill had a mare who had a foal every year. Bill came over one time and said there was trouble; the mare had had her foal and she couldn't get up on her feet. So Dad said, "We'll go over, we'll go over." And on the way over Dad said to him, "When she hears my voice outside, she'll jump up." And she did! And she was all right. A strange voice, you know. Got up to protect the foal.

John Fumerton was a smart man. He had a little livery stable, three horses, in Fallbrook years ago. And he had a stall in the stable with a board across about halfway up and he kept clay there and poured water into that. When a horse came in off the road his feet would be hot after hammering the road. That horse would stand in the wet clay and take the fever out of his feet. Now, they knew something about horses, didn't they?

The same for sprains and all; each had a different cure. That weed, tansy, they'd stew that into a good strong mixture and put that hot on a sprain on a horse. And that really is good. And for kidney trouble they used to place their fingers on a horse's back, just above the kidneys, and if he'd flinch that was a sign he had kidney trouble. They'd use saltpetre for that or two ounces of sweet nitre. Sometimes Dad used to buy a thin livery horse very reasonable, and he knew it had worms. He would take it home and give it two ounces of turpentine in a pint-and-a-half of raw linseed oil and boys, oh, boys, that would get rid of the worms. And help the horse! And if it wasn't doing too well, he'd bleed it and turn it out on the fresh grass in the spring. And you wouldn't know it in two months. Build it right up with new flesh.

There used to be an old lad — an old quack doctor — went around the country, bleeding horses and filing horses' teeth. One time Sam Shanks' boys came up from Cananto and they were at Bob North's on the Lanark Road and in comes this old lad. He wanted to know if they had any horses that needed their teeth filed. So these young lads, they went and got out their horse; they knew he had filed its teeth a couple of days before. So they got him to examine them. "Oh," he said, "Terrible altogether, oh, they need filing bad." So the young lads said, "You filed them two days ago." And he just got into the cart and away he went.

But horses' teeth need to be dressed sometimes. Some horses. You see, horses' teeth are not level at the top, they're sloped. They cut both ways and there are ridges along the outside of the horse's teeth, did you ever notice that? And on the inside. When they get grinding, some of these points won't wear and they have to be dressed down or they'd cut the cheeks or cut the tongue.

A blacksmith was a very important man in his community. He took his place. We remembered all those old remedies. Oh, I've sewed up horses after runaways and everything. A terror. And I've stopped horses bleeding to death, too, I've sewed them up. John Blair was loading manure with his team at the back of the barn. Mrs. Blair went around the corner of the barn — the team was still young — and they jumped and ran through an old disk harrow. My wife, Isobel, came over to the shop and said Blair's horses had run away and one was hurt bad; could I go?

The horse was lying down in the stall in a puddle of blood and his eyes were getting glassy and his breath was getting short. So I crawled in and oh, he was a kicking beggar to shoe. There was a squirt of blood coming out the size of a lead pencil, from an artery. I got a cotton sheet and tore off a strip eight inches wide, and tied a wide strip of cotton around, then rubbed flour in until the cloth was saturated, until it couldn't take any more. Then another strip, rubbed in more flour, and more flour, kept on and the horse got all right! The horse got all right.

Another time Bert Duncan was taking a bunch of cattle from his place up into Dalhousie to pasture and one of them tramped on a broken bottle or something in the ditch and was he ever bleeding! We got him into the blacksmith shop and we tried different things on it but the bleeding wouldn't stop. So I went around the windows and the corners of the shop and got a handful of cobwebs and put them on the cut and the bleeding stopped. I saw it happen. No explanation of it, but, I tell you, there's something in blood that makes it clot itself and maybe the webs around the cut got the blood to clot.

And the cures they had for heaves! Did you ever hear about them? The heaves in a horse is something like asthma in people. There were an awful lot of heavey horses in those days and everybody had a different cure. Some would gather up those old bunches of sumac, the red blossoms, and grind them up and mix them with

Walter's carving of a heavey horse

the horse's oats. I used to listen to them all and ask questions. Caused from feeding musty hay, the heaves.

Well, when the gypsies were coming around, that was *the* day! You people wouldn't remember the gypsies with the horses and wagons and the old ladies with the flounces on their skirts. Oh, there'd be maybe ten or fifteen wagons and horses and kids and dogs and everything, and we'd hear they were coming when they were two hours away. And the horse traders would be at our shop with their horses that they wanted to get rid of. The whole gang would be wondering when the gypsies would arrive. There'd be terrific excitement. And the horses they wanted to unload, a lot of them had the heaves. Big Harry Morrison had a temporary cure for the heaves — thirteen grains of shot. He'd put it down the horse's neck and in about twenty minutes there'd be no heaves but it would pretty soon wear off. Big Harry — he'd weigh three hundred and something — if he had a bad heaver somebody would go to the telephone. "Where are they now?" "Well, they're at Bell's Flats." "Oh, it'll be half an hour before they get here." So they'd phone again. "They're just on the other side of Foley's." "Oh, I'd say they should be here in about twenty minutes."

We had a couple of trestles, the big kind, and we'd get Harry up on them and I would hold the horse's head at just the right angle — I had a strong arm from blacksmithing — and when the gypsies were a few minutes away, Harry'd put the thirteen grains of shot down the horse's neck and then everybody'd stand back and watch! After a while the horse's heaves'd ease up and we'd take away the trestles. And then the gypsies would drift up. We'd have to lock the shop door or the old ladies would get in and steal everything in the shop. Oh, they had gowns on, full of pockets and everything. Wanted to tell our fortunes, you know.

I'd be watching the old gypsy man. Oh, if you ever saw a pair of eyes in anybody's head; he saw five times as much as anybody else could, looking everybody's horses over. And he could tell those fellows more about their horses than they knew themselves.

So they'd get into the dickering. Well, that was fun. Everybody wanted *boot*, you know. You know what boot is? Oh, that was a corker! Boot is, well, if you traded me a horse, I'd have to have something extra to boot. "Oh, no, no; you've got to give me two dollars, or something!" There'd be an exchange of the horses but everybody'd have to get a wee bit of money or, oh, maybe a bag of oats or a hen or potatoes, before they'd trade. Well, anyway, there would be three or four trades around. And then next morning they'd all look at what they got and it'd maybe be worse than what they had in the first place! Oh, terrible! Terrible! But they had to get rid of something and the

Walter and Andy in 1918

expression to boot is so old nobody thinks much about it anymore. Like forenenc't. What does forenenc't mean? In front of, I suppose.

We used to have those patent medicine shows, too, travelling from one community to another; they'd sell Indian snake oil and two cents' worth of peanuts for ten cents. There was one old lad, he'd eat the peanuts, shells and all. He got his money's worth!

Magic and Mischief

Do you believe in curses? Well, I know of a case, this happened about, oh, over sixty years ago. This family took scarlet fever or diphtheria or something and was quarantined and one of the neighbours was appointed to care for them, to help. And this old lad that was quarantined was not too happy about the bread he was brought. He told me that he had put a curse on the old man that brought it. At that time I didn't believe in it but not too long afterwards the elderly man fell at this lad's place and broke his leg and that leg was never right after. Another man was sent and it wasn't long before he got all stiffened up, all crippled up.

I knew people that had come from Ireland that believed in fairies. And did you ever hear stories about witches? I knew a family that believed in witches. The son had studied it. Oh, he was pretty good. He got these witch papers from the States and I'd read them to him. I don't know if I read them just right or not but I'd have him so terrified that he was afraid to hitch up his horse to go home.

This lad's team was always thin and worn out and they'd often get stuck on the road when they were drawing wood. He would get a gad and hit along the runners of the sleigh to chase the witches away. By the time he was finished the horses would be rested enough that they were ready to go again.

They got bothered pretty bad by witches another time and they had this hollow log they'd pulled up in front of the house, for firewood, you know. They all got around and chased the witches into the hollow log. After they'd rounded them up and hunted them all in they put a plug in the end of the log but they were so anxious to keep them in the log that they put the plug in too tight. Split the log and the witches got out on them. How they knew when they had them all in or when they'd all got out, I don't know. But, oh, you find out a lot if you listen to people.

Another time an old lady was churning cream, oh, churned for two or three days. Still no butter, so she took a fork and put it in the stove and got it red hot. Then she stuck it in the cream and the butter came. And the next day a poor old woman came along with a burn the size and shape of a fork on her hip. You see, the witch was supposed to be in the cream and that's why it wouldn't turn into butter.

Well, you know if you believe in it, it will come true!

A great many people can't understand or don't believe in people being able to read fortunes in tea leaves but I'll tell you a little story that happened about 1880. My grandfather and grandmother Wrathall and family lived in a very backward place up the 8th line. They got discouraged and a farm at Harper came up for sale. In those days a couple of thousand dollars was a terrible investment; everybody was afraid of debt. So they didn't know what to do.

Well, my grandparents decided that Grandfather should go down to see this Mother Barnes; she read teacups and a lot of people had great faith in what she told them. So he hitched up very early one morning with the horse and cutter and drove down to the third line and picked up his brother George on the Wrathall homestead and they drove down to Plum Hollow. It's a little place down towards Brockville, a long drive and when they got there they had to tie their horse to the fence and wait their turn.

My grandfather and his brother went in and they got the cup of tea and she tossed the cup — turned it around on the saucer, you know, to see how the tea leaves would settle. Then she read whatever she saw in them. She said, "You've left a very sick child at home today," and grandfather said, "Yes I did; Mary was very sick when I left; I didn't know whether I should come or not." "And," she said, "you have the opportunity of buying a farm and from what I see here you'd do well to go ahead and buy it. But you're going to pay fourteen dollars more than the price you were figuring on paying, but go ahead and buy it." And they did and they were well pleased with it all. They did have to pay another fourteen dollars because that was the bailiff's charge and the new owner had to pay that. Oh, this Barnes woman told people how to find lost children and about murders and everything else; they called her the witch of Plum Hollow. They say there was a play made up about her a few years back.

One night a bunch of us went down to Carleton Place to the Old Home Week. We got walking around and we came to a fortune teller and I said, "Come on in and get your fortune told." But the girl I was with said,

"Oh, no, no, I wouldn't go." So I said, "Well, come in — I want to get mine told." At that time I hadn't settled down to anything, going out with different people. So this old lady, Madam Zedda, said "You have two sisters and one brother." "Yes, that's right." "And you're a mechanic." "Oh," I said, "a kind of a one, a kind of a one." She said, "Your father is a lot older than your mother." "Yes." "Inside of nine months you're going to be married." And I said, "Well, what kind of a lady am I going to get?" "You're going to marry a lady with dark hair, a high complexion and an oval-shaped face. And, inside of fifteen months you're going to be running another business." "Oh," I said, "And am I going to quit what I'm at now?" and she said, "No, you're not, you're going to run the two of them!" And, by golly, it came true. It came true! Oh, I dunno; things like that make you wonder.

Oh, it's funny how things happen. One Perth Fair day, in September, I took my mother into town with the horse and buggy and I let her out to see the programme. I said, "I'll put the horse in the stable and I'll catch up to you."

So I put the horse in and I was travelling down the street and I met Mrs. John Blair and I stopped for a minute. She gave me an introduction to this young lady with them — oh, a very nice introduction — this was Miss Isobel Blair, her husband's cousin, and I was the village blacksmith. I was just ... by golly, I liked the looks of her! I just thought to myself going down the street, "She's just as good looking as they said she was!" So I caught up to Mother and we went to the fair, and when the fair was over I drove Mother home to Fallbrook.

Isobel — she told me this later, you know — Isobel went home with her brother with the horse and buggy and when they got home it was late and her father and mother had gone to bed. She said, instead of going up to her room she went to her father and mother's room for a little chat and she told them, "I met a man in Perth today and I'd like to ask him to this house." "Well," her father said. "Who is he?" "His name's Walter Cameron. He's a blacksmith at Fallbrook, but Fallbrook has a kind of a tough name." And it did at that time. Her father thought it over and he said,

"Well, I was at his father and mother's wedding; I know all his mother's people and I knew his father's brother, Watty, who ran the hotel at Fallbrook. They're all good people; you ask him."

So she found a way, she found a way, and that didn't make me mad! Oh, I'd heard about her often; I'd got some great reports on her and I'd talked to some reliable people about her and I'd just been getting pretty anxious to meet her.

Well, I used to drive out there with this little grey horse, Andy, to see my wife — well, she wasn't my wife then — I guess I called her Miss at first, right on the start it was Miss, but it was Isobel shortly! Oh, she was a wonderful person in that community; so many times I'd be introduced to somebody out there later and they'd say, "This is the lad that came out here and stole the best lady in our whole community!"

On the 15th day of April, 1925, I married Isobel Blair, one of the finest people I ever knew. We were married in the Anglican church at Brook and we went on a honeymoon to Niagara Falls where every bride and groom went in those days.

Tales from the Candy Counter

It's a strange thing the way we started with the store. One day Jim Geary came into the shop and he said, "Would you sell me your house?" I said, "Well, if we'd someplace to go we'd sell. I don't care where we live." "Well, if you take a notion, let me know," he said. And, by golly, two days after, the man from the store, Jimmy Campbell, came over and said, "Have you any notion of buying our store? We're going to sell it." I asked him the price and he told me and I asked if he'd take two or three hundred less. "Well," he said, "I'll just go over and talk to my wife about it." So he was back in about ten minutes and he said, "Yes, we'll take your offer."

You know my wife was just ideal for a store so I bought it right there. I went home at dinnertime from the blacksmith shop and I said, "I just bought the store." That's the way it went; we moved in, in October, 1925. The house and the store were all in one building. And there was the second business!

Isobel had worked for ten years at Brook with her aunt and oh, she did love a store! She knew the value of everything from the time she was a young girl. I tell you, she was a woman who could make an advantage out of a disadvantage; she was a born storekeeper. I think everybody has a groove to fit into if they just know when to accept it. And watch and listen. I had an aunt run a store one time and she said if you're losing business in something, keep your ear to the ground and you'll learn.

Our little Margaret was born on the 16th day of May in 1927 and she was just a perfect child, very much like her mother in her disposition and her ways but she was built more like me. But she was like Isobel in so many ways. Isobel blushed very easily and little Margaret was the very same. I would say to her, "I know where there's a pretty, pretty little girl," and she'd blush right back to the back of her neck. Isobel said she just watched for me all the time and the day she took that disease, pyelitis, she was just beginning to walk. Her mother had her on a little mat in the dining room and she was practicing getting up and down. She got up and she was walking away from me. She wanted to see if I was watching her and she turned around and lost her balance. She just laughed and laughed; a very happy child. But from that day on she was sick with that awful disease; sometimes her temperature would go to 105 and 106. We took her to different doctors and we brought her to the baby specialist in Kingston but they couldn't do anything for her. She had to go and she died the last day of May in 1928 — just a little over a year old. There were three others around that had that disease at that same time.

Then on the 13th of January, 1930 Graham was born. We named him James Graham Cameron and I say yet he's the finest man I ever knew. I

Walter's parents with his daughter, Margaret Elizabeth, in 1928

don't know of a thing that Graham ever did that didn't please me. Then he married a very fine woman; if he'd been looking until now he couldn't have found a better wife than June. And their three children, I can't see a thing wrong with them and it's my ambition now for the rest of my time to do things to please every one of them. I often think of the wonderful life Graham and I have had and I used to wonder if a father and son ever had the relationship we have but now I can see it in his own family; they have the same kind of relationship. Graham was quite a philosopher even when he was a young lad; he used to say to me, "Dad, never make up your mind on anything until all of the facts are in." And isn't that good advice?

When we had the store, along with the blacksmith shop, Graham and I were in Perth one morning with the truck; Graham was about ten years old. We were in James Brothers hardware store and Johnny Duncan from the McEwen Line came in; he was always in a hurry and he said, "Walter, are you near through here?" I said, "I'm through now, Johnny. Why?" "Well, I want you to look at a car down the street."

The three of us walked up the street and came to this car. Johnny said, "What do you think of that?" "Well," I said, "Johnny, I don't know much about cars but," I said, "we have one at home that looks a lot like it." "That's it. I bought it from your wife coming in," he says, "You've some papers in your pocket belonging to it." So! We were without a car, then but that's the way we did business!

I went in for dinner one day and my wife said, "I sold your rubbers today." I said, "That's fine." She said, "There was a man who came along here and we didn't have the right size for him and you only had those on two or three times. And," she said, "I wish there was more in there we could sell."

Oh, she was a great worker and did she ever love to buy and sell. She'd had a good training with her aunt and she did love a store. We bought that store in 1925 and we had it for thirty years, all through the Great Depression, you know, and people that I knew all my life would come in. "We haven't a pound of flour in the house," or "The boys have no rubbers to go to school." We did business by saying "What have you got for us?" Some winters we'd have five thousand cords of wood, cord wood, pulp, stove wood, everything, that we'd taken in on trade. Carloads of it!

My wife, Isobel, would just make up a contract with them and say, "Now, that's good up to a hundred dollars," and they'd go ahead and buy a hundred dollars' worth and they'd bring carloads of wood or I took carloads of horses up to Montreal!

Oh, she was a great sales lady! She'd sell people things and they'd hardly know they were buying, very quiet. But she just had that magic.

But oh, with all our business — the blacksmith shop and the general store — we got a great insight into human nature. The old lads'd sit around on the counter or around the stove in the winter time and tell stories. The stories that were told in the store were a little more refined than some of the ones told at the blacksmith shop.

We kept the store open weeknights until nine or ten o'clock. Saturday nights when they'd be going away they'd say, "Well, we'll see you next Saturday." Oh, there'd be people on the verandah and everywhere. When the store got too crowded Isobel would just have them wander into the house part; the women would go in there to try on dresses, too. One Saturday night we served fifty-four families from six to quitting time, eleven or twelve o'clock.

Did I ever tell you about the experience we had with a man taking candy at our store? This man would half sit up on the counter, right close to the peppermints. And he'd be feasting on these peppermints and in the way at the counter. My wife wouldn't like to be complaining about it but I knew she didn't like it. So I said, "All right, leave it to me!" I took the flat peppermints out and I put these Scotch ones in, the round ones, and boy, did he ever go to town on them! I left them there a day or two till he got really well acquainted with them and then I took them out and put mothballs in. So! We knew he'd be along.

He had a moustache about as long as your finger. So we got out of sight and he put a couple of them in his mouth and sat up. I went down and started telling him a story, a lo-o-o-ng story! And I could see a queer expression coming into his eyes so I

kept the story going and his cheeks started coming out and his eyes got wild! I kept on with this story and he couldn't swallow, he couldn't spit, his mouth was just getting full of it. So he made a bound outside to spit and he turned sick; oh, vomited something terrible! And he wasn't pleased about it, you know! Now, wasn't that a good idea to cure him?!

The Motor Age Arrives

There was a lot of excitement around here when people got cars first. Nobody knew anything about them. A lot of the dealers that sold them didn't know much about them either. Well, one day Fred Malotte went into Perth and he bought a car. I never heard of another kind with the same name; Flanders, or something like that. Well, they got it started and got Fred into it and away he went! They didn't tell him how to stop it or do anything else so Fred got home and he kept trying all the wee gadgets but he couldn't get it stopped. Finally he guided it around and ran it up against a tree — it wouldn't be going very fast — and he stopped it that

Cars and people last a long time in Fallbrook

way! He wasn't going to run it all day. Somebody came along after a while and Fred shouted, "Pat, how the heck do you stop these things where's there's no tree?"

The use of the horses was pushed out by the cars coming in. But the blacksmiths got very nicely eased out of it. But those old cars, a lot of funny things happened when the cars came out! People would come into the blacksmith shop and tell us the luck they had, getting in and out from town and meeting no cars, or meeting them at a laneway where they could drive in with the horses till the car got by.

When I was a young fellow, I was up at McKerrecher's store one day and a woman and her mother-in-law came down with the horse and buggy and they just got the horse tied up and got nicely into the store and Mrs. McKerrecher started using the sewing machine upstairs. The old lady jumped up and shouted, "What was that?" I said, "Oh, that's a car going by," so she hurried to do her business and it got quiet again. Then Mrs. McKerrecher would run another seam and the old lady would start up again. "Just another car," I said, "going to the lake, I guess." Well sir, the old lady started to swear and she stayed there for I don't know how long thinking there was a bunch of cars going through. Finally they rushed out to get away and home, between cars, you know!

But then, after a while some of the younger horses and younger people got used to them; the older horses and older people rebelled right to the last. When you wanted to buy a road horse they'd guarantee that he'd "eat oats out of an autocar." That was the guarantee! Oh, a lot of funny things happened; they should have been recorded years ago!

When you get older you get thinking about the sayings of the old people. Mother used to say, "There never was an old shoe but there's a mate for it." And there was an old Geary man lived across the road from us and he lived to be nearly ninety! I heard him say one time that he was going to live as long as he saw anybody else living!

Isobel and I had a lovely life together. She had a wonderful disposition you know, never saw it change, never saw it change. We lived in the store from 1925 to 1955. We started to build the other house, the one I'm in now, in 1952; tried to sell the store but those days nobody wanted a store and it took a while. We built the new house by our own plans and everything then we just had three-and-a-half years in it together. We thought we were all set. We had everything arranged for two to run and I do it in half a way now. But I think I'm doing exactly what Isobel would have wanted me to do. I'm keeping at the blacksmithing too, in a small way. I make trivets and lucky horseshoes and things like that and I whittle in my spare time. Oh, never idle, never idle!

Walter and Isobel in their new house in 1957

5
Conversation with an Octogenarian

The Woodcarver

I always liked to whittle; I really don't know when I started but I did always love a jackknife from the time I can remember. Any spare money I earned I invested in a good knife. Then, when we sold the store in 1955 and I could start to whittle and do carving, I found fifteen good jackknives that I had put away when I was a boy. If I showed you my favourite knife you'd think I should throw it in the bush. In the early 1900s, anybody lucky enough to have a genuine Boeker was envied by all his chums. I bought one almost seventy years ago and it's still one of my favourite whittling tools.

Billy Lee from the Ninth Line used to come over to my dad's blacksmith shop to get his horse shod. While he was waiting he would talk to me and my brother; he was a man who always had time to talk to a boy. I can appreciate that now — and I did then! When he was a young man he spent some winters working at the lumber camp, the shanty, up north. He'd tell us about an old man who used to whittle chains at nights and on Sundays at the lumber camp. He explained to me about the links and from his description I whittled a chain with a cage and two wooden balls in it when I was ten or twelve years old. Then, oh, for years I didn't get a chance to whittle but it was still bothering me.

When we moved over into the new

Everything in the miniature blacksmith's shop is one-twelfth life size

house, I got going, found these knives and got some good basswood and started to whittle. And I've had whittle-itis ever since. And I hope it's catching! All you have to do is to take off the right amount of wood in the right places. You have to have an imagination and I guess it helps a little if you can draw. You see, I like to figure out the object in my mind before I start and sometimes I sketch it first.

My first love was horses so to start, I carved a bunch of them. When I was shoeing horses, I used to tell my customers, "A horse is only half a horse if he's not shod," so then I had to live up to that and I made up my mind I was going to shoe the little horses I carved.

I got some Swedish iron, hammered it out to the size for a tiny shoe and bent it. Then I had to make the little tools to put the crease in for the nail heads and then I made the nails. The first horse I shod was a dapple grey mare but oh, I didn't get as good a job as I would have liked so I sold it to a man, told him I didn't like the shoeing. I kept on and kept getting better at it all the time; my father taught me to be a perfectionist. Now I've got two Arab horses with hind feet only about nine-sixteenths of an inch across. I made the shoes for them, put the creases in, made the nails and nailed them on. I was very well pleased with them so from then on I just shod every horse I carved.

Well, I kept on with my horses; I had about twenty and they were all shod but one. I made an Arab from a picture I saw in a horseman's book; this picture was about two inches by one-and-three-quarter and it was of a horse belonging to some big abdullah in Persia or someplace; he'd presented it to the president of the United States. I studied that picture until I knew every joint in it and the proportions of it all the way through. Those Arabian horses have wonderful eyes; they see so much and I studied those eyes and all until I could picture him standing out in the yard in the flesh. Then I took my pencil and drew his picture standing there, cut it out with a bandsaw and carved and whittled until I got it just right. I have two like that; one I think is the best horse I ever carved and I'm giving that to my granddaughter, Janet. I have three grandchildren, two boys and one girl and the boys don't seem to care one hoot about horses; you'd never know there was a horse! But Janet does dearly love a horse and she likes a white or a grey horse as I did so I'm giving her that.

There is an old saying, "To want is a keener pleasure than to have," and I tell people I've had four different kinds of pleasure out of doing that. I've had the pleasure of wanting to do that horse for her, the pleasure of carving it for her, the pleasure of giving it to her and the pleasure of knowing that she'll always have it as a remembrance of me.

In my carvings of horses, I benefited from understanding and studying the horses I shod; I knew what they were thinking and you can see that in my horses' eyes. You know there's just as many differences in horses as there are in people. And here's something foolish I'm going to tell you: I can see the same characteristics in horses as I can in people. Now you take the formation of a face; there's every design in a horse's face and there's every design in a person's face. You see people that, the first time you see them, you're not too happy about them; horses are the same. There is just as much difference in a horse's eyes as there is in a man's eyes, and in the formation of the head. Some horses are shallow at the back of the jaws and heavy at the nostrils; we used to call them "the barnyard lunk." No brains whatever, no brains whatever!

Then people started asking me, "Have you ever tried carving cows?" "No, never tried any cows." So Isobel and I went and studied some Jerseys and some Ayrshires and some Guernseys and I got interested in carving cattle. We would go to the fall fairs and sit on bales of straw or hay and study the type of cow I was carving; I'd do some sketching and what I missed, Isobel noticed. I have a Jersey bull — and they are a ferocious kind of animal, can't be trusted for a minute — and I've got that wild, fighting look right in his eyes. Then, to show the contrast, I carved the cow and her eyes show against the other's; the eyes of the cow are so gentle and kind, like a deer's eyes.

In my collection I have a pair of good Ayrshires, a Guernsey cow and a Holstein. Harry Mather had about twenty-two milk cows out in a field not too far from where I live. One day I said, "Harry, if you see a strange-looking guy walking around among your cows, don't shoot; I'm going out

some day to do some sketches." And afterwards Harry asked me, "Did you sketch the cow? Which one did you do?" And I said, "Harry, I just took them all apart and I sketched what I liked in one and what I liked in another until I thought I had a perfect Holstein cow."

Then the film people came along to do this film *Knacky People* and they had me go out with the cameras on me and go through this same performance. I sat on a stone pile and sketched the cows and I came home and carved one out and I'm very happy about this model.

People are always asking me why I don't get a television set. Now, if I'd been watching television every night that I've done this whittling what would I have? Nothing! And I've been on TV, oh, I don't know how many times; some of the shows have been all over the country. When they ask why I don't want a television I tell them I can think of enough foolish things myself. I tell the TV fellows I'm not old enough yet to be entertained; I want to be educated! Is there anything wrong with that? Anyway, I'm just eighty-four and I haven't time to watch television.

I was asked to do a carving of a team of prize drawers, horses that won prizes at hauling heavy loads. These people in the States brought the pictures up; one was a strawberry roan and the other a blue roan; powerful horses. The strawberry roan toed in very badly which is a good sign in a heavy drawing team; they can draw a lot more if they toe in than if they toe out. I got a real good job on his front feet and I got his eyes perfect, but it took a lot of experimenting to get the paint to bring out the strawberry roan colour.

You see, a strawberry roan horse is a chestnut with every second hair white and the other chestnut coloured, so that was kind of hard to mix paints to get it just right. But I got that beat and I was very happy about it. Got him shod perfectly and everything. Then the other was a blue roan and that was another challenge; how can you get that colour? You can't send to Eaton's catalogue for it. But I got it perfect, by trial and error. There was nobody I could go and ask because I don't know anybody who paints roan horses. So I'm very proud of that and pleased to have them in my collection.

One time my sister took a picture
of my son Graham in front of Father's
house; he'd just come home from
fishing and he'd caught a few fish, you
know, with an old gad of a fishing
pole. He was, oh, eight or ten and he
was pretty proud of those fish he'd
caught. The picture was three or four
inches high and two-and-a-half or
three inches the other way.

Graham Cameron

Well, I took a notion to carve him
and in the carving he's about ten
inches tall. This was a very particular
one and I got his face and his stature
and everything perfect; toenails on
the toes and fingernails on the
fingers. And I have him smiling. I
painted him just like he was, the old
blue suit the little boys wore at that
time. A few years ago I had a bunch
of visitors from London, Ontario, and
one was a trained sculptor. He looked
at it for a long time, then he said,
"You're not a whittler, you're not a
carver, you're a sculptor." And I said,
"Mister, why did you say that?"
"Well," he said, "Anybody that can
take a block of wood and make it
smile as a little boy smiles and put
expression in wood, he is a sculptor!"

Another thing I'm very proud of is
my miniature blacksmith shop. When
people come to see my carvings I like
to take them into the old blacksmith
shop first; it's been there for 114
years and I'm still doing some work in
it. I will have been sixty years
blacksmithing in that shop in June,
1979; I started work on the seventh
day of June, 1912, with my father.
The shop has been in his name and
mine for ninety-one years.

The anvil in the old shop is two feet long and four generations of Camerons have hammered on that . . anvil. I forged the little one on that old one and it's two inches long. I made the forge as the original one was, a stone forge with the old-fashioned bellows that pumped to keep the fire going.

Then I whittled a work bench, an old tattered bench, with three drawers that would pull out and a leg vise that reached down to the floor. I scaled it an inch to the foot and I hammered it out on the anvil. It's a perfect replica of the old one; when you turn the handle it will open and close as the big one did. Where the big vise is six inches across the jaws, the little one is half an inch; one-twelfth the size and it's perfect. There's an old drill in it, too, for boring holes in iron, in buggy tires and so on. You had to turn a crank and bore the hole. The drill is whittled out in wood but the anvil and the vise are hammered out of steel.

Where the old blacksmith shop is twenty-four feet, the replica is twenty-four inches; I have windows with bars on, iron bars as they were in the old shop; the bars were put on the inside of the windows to keep the horses from breaking the glass. On the floor of the little shop I have tiny tools, the same as were used in the shop for 114 years. I have little pinchers for pulling the shoes off; where the big ones for removing the shoes from the real horses are about fourteen inches long, the little ones are about one-and-an-eighth inches long. They work just perfectly; just a perfect replica of the big pinchers. I have hammers and hoof clippers and I have the barrel for holding the wheel on to do the woodwork, all whittled out, and I have two wagon wheels with the tires off in front of the shop. Those wheels are about four inches in diameter. Each wheel is whittled out of one piece of wood with bands on the hubs as there were bands on the hubs on the old wagon wheels. There are tongs for holding the hot shoes, too, and other different types of hammers; cold sets and hot sets; oh, the whole setup.

I have a full blacksmith outfit in miniature and I've been told many times by people who have travelled the world over that there's not another like that little building in the world. It took me three weeks to make wooden shingles and put them on the roof and to make the old chimney to come through, black and sooty looking. The rough floor, the wooden floor, is just like the one I worked on for years and years.

I'm especially proud of the carvings of the three of us; I have my father sitting on a horseshoe keg, watching me shoe our little horse, Andy. People who knew my father say that if I whittled a replica of him a thousand

times I could not improve on his posture, his head and back and hands, the way he sat, every particular, with the old-fashioned police braces, a handkerchief hanging out of one pocket and a rule sticking out of the other. He's watching me and I have my leather apron on, shoeing a hind foot. The horse has his head turned around to the side I'm working on, as horses do when you're shoeing that foot. And the horse's eye is looking right at me and that expression of a horse standing, waiting is right in his eyes and ears. Sitting on a cheese box close by is my son, Graham, when he was a little boy, in his bare feet. He's eating an apple and the horse is sniffing, waiting for that apple core.

So I have three generations of our family in my little blacksmith shop,

along with a perfect replica of that little grey horse. He and I were young together and he was a faithful friend of mine. When we were coming home, at nights, through storms and snowdrifts I'd often say to him, "Andy, what can I ever do to repay you for what you're doing for me?" Now, if this little shop and everything that's in it goes into a museum, I wonder if there's any horse ever got a higher honour? And he deserved it.

When I went into Perth on a Saturday night, if I had a little time I liked to drive in to Tom Devlin's. He was a horse dealer in Perth and he handled thousands of horses, thousands of them. I liked to have a look at his horses. I'd leave Andy hitched to the buggy in the yard, nobody holding him, and he'd stand there until I came out. If there were some people around Tom would always ask me to unhitch him and show what tricks he could do. So I'd take him out, take every strap off him and he'd go through his tricks, shake hands and all that. And when he'd finish I'd put the harness back on and put the lines in the turrets and walk around and throw the halter into the buggy. Before I could throw that halter into the buggy, he'd swing right around and in between the shafts. Hundreds of people used to watch him; he'd do anything I said. I thought he deserved the honour of being in the miniature blacksmith shop. Oh, that little white horse has been seen by a lot of people.

The little building's made out of old barn lumber and I put special windows in it that slide; glass in the windows and frames and everything. I like to get people to look in at the end of the little blacksmith shop and tell them to notice that the little windows aren't set in straight; if they were straight in an old building, it wouldn't look right.

I went to a lot of trouble to catch spiders to have cobwebs in the little shop as they are in the old shop. And I had them beautiful! And one day, I don't know whether to say a lady or not, but somebody who *could not stand cobwebs*, took her hand and wiped them right out! And that did not please me!

We never had a sign on the old blacksmith shop because everybody for twenty miles in every directio᷄ knew it, but I have my sign, "Walter Cameron, Blacksmith," on the little

84

shop as a remembrance. I put a little horseshoe with the heels turned down above the name; you see, a horseshoe above a blacksmith's shop door should be turned with the open end down to let the luck run into the forge; anywhere else it's turned up to hold the luck in.

I made a little stone, an imitation of the big stone where we used to set the wagon tires. This stone was about six feet across and there was a hole in the centre about fifteen or sixteen inches in diameter. The hub of these big wagon wheels would go down in the hole and the wheel would lie flat on that stone. Then we would heat the tire and when we got it the right size we'd put it on the wooden wheel and then put water on to keep it from burning the wood. I've got that replica of the old stone and I've got the pump, an old wooden pump with a trough right beside it, for getting water to cool the tire. That was a hot old job, hammering and swinging the sledge with a great big fire on to heat that tire. Boy, that was a hot job!

Oh, there's a lot of memories right there in that little blacksmith shop; I did enjoy the hours I spent carving that; a kind of memorial to my profession and something very special to leave. I like to think someday my grandchildren will look at it in a museum and say, "My grandfather did that!"

I have another carving that means an awful lot to me; I call it "A Message from Beyond." My wife came to me in a dream one night, two-and-a-half years after she died. She held up this little six-sided object with a ball loose inside, showed how the ball worked in it and smiled and disappeared. The next day I started to carve those little cubes for Isobel's friends and I made a lot of them. Isobel still comes to me in dreams; she doesn't talk but I seem to get the message every time.

The tall object is a thingamajig

85

Oh, all my carvings aren't serious. I've done a few foolish ones too, some political cartoons, an old heavey horse and so on. But, in everything I do, I strive for a perfect likeness, whether it's an old horse with the heaves or a purebred Clydesdale. And I think everybody should have a few thing-a-ma-jigs in the house. Look at this: if you turn it sideways it's a thing-a-ma-bob and if you hold it upside down it's a what-cha-ma-call-it. Oh, once a man, twice a boy, you know!

Some Things Should Not Be Forgotten...

People built up this country using oxen. They say that those tremendous stones at the locks on the Rideau Canal were all brought in with oxen. Now I'm making hundreds of ox shoes, the way they were made 150 years ago and I'm putting them on plaques to give the oxen credit for what they did. And when people buy these plaques with the ox shoes on, some of them say they never knew oxen wore shoes! The oxen did a lot of work for this country up until about 1867, when the farmers pretty well switched over to horses. But you see, an ox, when working on the road, his feet would wear down and he couldn't work on ice without shoes. I still have some of the shoes that were worn by oxen in the old days.

Sawyer Jim Cameron had a yoke of oxen. He had grown up out at Wemyss and they had a big swamp with heavy elm in it. Timber buyers used to come up the Tay River and they had powerful teams, oh, tremendous horses. Whoever sold them the logs would have to bring them out of the swamp and put them on a skid or something. Then these people with the big teams would back the front sleigh under the logs and chain it on and trail it over to the river.

Well, Jim's father cut this big elm, it was about sixty feet long, and he skidded it out with the oxen; then the buyers came up the river and hitched onto it. By golly, they couldn't stir it with their horses and they had to get Jim's father to hitch onto it again with his oxen and bring it out to the river. I asked Jim, "How heavy would those oxen be?" "Well," he said, "they got to the place where they had to get rid of them and they put the crop in

A horseshoe and an ox shoe, made by Walter Cameron

with them that spring, then they turned them out to grass. In the fall one weighed 1,900 pounds and the other 2,000!" Oh, they were powerful animals!

Some of the older men that went to the lumber camp said the horse teamsters sat at one end of the shanty and the men that drove the yokes of oxen sat at the other end. They claimed that there was a different odour off them. You see, skidding the logs out, getting mixed up with the chains and everything, the oxen weren't particular!

In the olden days when they wanted to train a pair of calves for a team they would start when they were a year old and they'd make a little yoke and put it on the calves and they'd have them on all winter. They'd get used to staying together

and then they'd go out to grass in the spring and when they came in in the fall again, they'd put a bigger yoke on, let them go around all winter with that yoke on and then, when they were coming on three years old, they were ready to work them, sometimes sooner, depending on their size. Oxen were usually called Buck and Bright.

But imagine, people heading to town with a yoke of oxen, sitting on an old ox cart, five or six hours on the road. Some of those big yokes were ten inches deep and five or six inches the other way, tapered off at the top. A lot depended on how oxen were broken in, how they were driven, from a cart, walking ahead of them or at the side of them. Some people called it "walking the oxen."

Did you ever see that big bandwagon that's at Upper Canada Village with James Brothers printed on the side of it? Do you know the history of it? Well, that circus outfit, Barnum and Bailey, broke down in Perth and George James' father was a blacksmith and he did a lot of work for them. He took that bandwagon in payment and then it was handed down to George.

On big days in town George used to

hire a team to take people for rides. Well, then Upper Canada Village wanted it and he came out to me one night and he said, "Would you tell me what you think about it?" "Well, do you want to know exactly what I think? I've sat in that bandwagon on your tours and if something frightened those horses that aren't used to it and people got hurt, who would be responsible?" "You know," he says, "I never thought of that!" And he gave it to them. I think he was glad to get that responsibility off his mind.

When Hugh and I were young lads there wasn't the entertainment the kids have today and in the summer evenings we'd often just sit on the big verandah after our lessons were done and listen to the cow bells all through the country. Each bell had a different sound and it was musical. They say the first cow bells sold in this part of the country were made in Brockville by a blacksmith and there were a lot of them used; they made it easier to keep track of the cows when they were in the bush. Usually the lead cow wore a bell and the rest pretty well followed her.

I remember too when we used to go on our bare feet until we were near the church on Sundays, then we had to squeeze our feet into boots. We went barefoot all summer and when we were going for the cows in the cool mornings we'd warm our bare feet by standing where the cows had been lying all night; the grass would be warm, you know. We went barefoot until the weather got too cold. By fall our toes were spread so far apart you could spit through them!

Did I tell you about the time they went to repair that bridge in Fallbrook? It was built, oh, away back in the 1820s and it started to go in the 1880s. So the council inspected it and decided to call a meeting to give everybody a chance to bid on repairs. They advertised in the paper and the people who were interested came. At that time Jim Anderson's mother had rented to a man by the name of John Toffee; he made cheese boxes. Toffee was quite a man to do business and he came to the meeting. The reeve got up and explained it all; the bridge needed new stringers and new covering, and the railing repaired. The stringers are the long pieces that go across.

"Now," Mr. Corey, the reeve, said,

"I'm open for bids. Make me an offer to do that job!" Toffee says, "I'll do it for thirty dollars." "Well," Corey says, "Mr. Toffee has offered to do the job for thirty dollars. Is there anybody can beat that bid?" And this old fellow gets up and says, "Thirty-one!" Mr. Corey says, "Lookit, we're not trying to bid higher; we want you to beat Mr. Toffee's bid. I'll take another bid." The old lad hops up again; "Thirty-two!" "Oh," the reeve says, "you're going the wrong way. Mr. Toffee will do the job for thirty dollars; you've got to beat that bid. I'll take another bid from you." The old fellow shouts "Thirty-three!" He was used to auction sales! So Mr. Corey said, "Mr. Toffee's got the job."

This same old lad was around when they were fixing the bridge and one day Mrs. Harry Bain who lived at the tollgate came by with her cow. Everybody kept a cow in the village at that time and a lot of them ran on the road. They'd torn all the covering off the bridge and that morning Mrs. Bain wanted to get her cow across the bridge and there were just the stringers there. So she asked this old fellow if she could get her cow over and he said, "Well, Mrs. Bain, if you

want to get that cow across the bridge, it will be at your own possibility!"

People didn't drive into Perth every day to get things! One day a woman from MacDonald's Corners came out to visit my mother when my aunt from Perth was visiting at our place. This woman had worked for

Isobel, Graham and Walter Cameron in 1935

Auntie up at the hotel here when she was a young girl. And oh, they were having a great visit. Auntie said, "Why don't you come in and visit me some day, Mrs. MacDonald?" They didn't use first names so much then, you know. "Well, I will," she said, "we're figuring on going into town some day this fall and I'll visit you then." Now imagine that, planning months ahead for a day in Perth!

Every patron of the cheese factory, in the olden days, had to take a load of cheese into town, that was in the agreement. There was quite a bit of cheese, sometimes two or three wagon loads at a time. They shipped it on Fridays so they'd get the team shod, maybe the wagon tires set, grease the old wagon the day before, come down in the morning and get the cheese loaded at the factory. Maybe they'd let one of the young lads go to town with them and that was a big day! They'd think more of that than we'd think of going to Montreal now. Shipped the cheese from Perth every Friday. The cheese buyers would be there from Brockville, waiting at the station sheds.

There used to be an old fellow in the back country who was always talking about getting married and he sent to the States for one of these papers on matrimony. These ladies would advertise with pictures, you know. But he couldn't read or write so he would get me to write letters for him. I don't know whether I wrote the way he wanted me to or not but, boy, there was a lot of correspondence! He never did get himself a wife but it's not everybody who can have a private secretary! Oh, I wasn't an expert but you know what they say about experts: "An expert is a handy man from out of town." Doesn't it seem that way?

Years ago we used to find those old wild plums and they made the nicest preserves we ever got; they had a flavour all their own. You'd find them in the corners of fences and the old people used to say the deer were very fond of them; they'd go and eat a whole lot of these plums and spit out the stones and then lie there and chew their cud and that started another cluster of red plum trees. You hardly see wild plums anymore; there was a kind of a blight got started in them and oh, I was sorry about that! They were wonderful, no taste quite the same, no taste quite the same!

People used a lot of wild fruit in earlier days. There were no refrigerators, no freezers or anything like that, but most of the old houses had good, cool basements and the women preserved a lot. One summer, when we had the store, there was a big, big blueberry crop and Billy Bedore had bought a lot of blueberries to sell to the stores. Billy was from above Ardoch, near a bridge across the Mississippi, and was a great customer of ours; he was the one that had brought the big bar to be welded.

Well, one Saturday morning, Billy was coming down to Perth to sell blueberries and on the way down somebody told him he wouldn't sell any blueberries in Perth, there were too many coming in. So he landed at our store with ninety-three, ten-quart pails of blueberries in his old truck made from a Model T Ford car. Billy and Isobel came over to the blacksmith shop to ask me what I thought about buying them. "Well now," I said, "if you want to buy them I'll do what I can to help you to sell them." Billy gave Isobel a pretty good price on them and she took them all. That night she hadn't a blueberry or a pound of sugar or a glass sealer left in the store. Well, she was happy about that — she did enjoy that store!

My mother taught us to laugh; oh a wonderful woman and a good neighbour. She used to churn butter twice a week and she took the buttermilk to an old deaf lady. The old woman always emptied the milk from the pail into a beautiful jug and before she died she gave the jug to my mother; it's still in the family. My mother had a lot of good neighbours and friends; May Burnham was one of them and she became a good friend of Isobel too; used to come and help her out when she needed extra help. May used to be in getting milk three or four times a week and I asked her the other day if she ever remembered going into Mother's house when Mother's hands were not busy doing something; knitting or making quilts or making a mat or something. I think my mother was the most contented woman I ever knew. I've seen little kids and older people going up onto the verandah to talk to her. She used to sit on the verandah in the summer a lot as she got older and she'd often say the sweetest music to her ears was the sound of my hammer on the anvil at the blacksmith shop. Oh, everybody liked my mother.

Mrs. Willis lived across the road and one year she and my mother were raising a pig each. Mother had a pig over at the barn and Mrs. Willis had a pig at their place. They used to be comparing notes; they'd go back and forth looking at the pigs and just having a nice friendly time. One day Mrs. Willis came to look at Mother's pig; they were in the barn talking away. I slipped around; the door had blown shut and I just hooked it closed. When they got through talking one went to push the door open and oh, dear, the door was stuck. Mother said, "We won't get out of here till Jim comes to feed the pig and that will be an hour and I've got bread in the oven!" Then Mrs. Willis was getting excited. "Well," Mother said, "Wait now and I'll call Cora." Cora lived at the store at that time. So Mother got her mouth up to the crack of the door and she called Cora. Cora came out and looked all around but she couldn't see anybody so she went back in again. "Well," Mrs. Willis said, "I'm taller than you; I can reach up closer to the opening." So she called and Cora came out again,

looked all around and went back in. Well, they were in desperation, they were clean sunk, so I thought they had punishment enough and I slipped around and took the hook off the door. They blamed it on the wind and I never told them any different.

The Wisdom of a Lifetime

People ask me a lot about the changes since I was a boy. "Well," I tell them, "for one thing I've noticed, people don't listen anymore; they don't listen and they don't hear. The old people listened and they remembered. Now if you read the papers, listened to the radio or watched television, you wouldn't have any convictions, would you? Everything's thought out for you. What the old fellows thought, they *really* thought. They had to think for themselves; they had very strong convictions. Oh, I tell you, if you aren't learning something all the time you're standing still."

I was visiting a friend of mine in the lumber business one time and I said to him, "It's wonderful to see so much going on here; so few men but everything going so smoothly; you must have a great way of handling your business." And he said, "Well, you know Mr. Cameron, so many people now have their heads full of a lot of little nothings."

Many of the old people had those old-fashioned sayings and as I get older they come back to me. Bill Warwick lived alone, away back from the main road, and he did a lot of thinking. You do a lot of thinking when you live alone. He had an expression he used if somebody said something about putting off a job or if he thought they were missing an opportunity; Bill would say: "The water only passes the mill once, so *g-r-r-ind*!" Scottish, you know.

I'm glad I'm as old as I am; we had our own lives to live and we got

Walter Cameron and Audrey Armstrong

along. We were all the same, like the old lady and the potatoes: "Our potatoes are no good this year but thank goodness nobody else's are either!"

There have been a lot of changes since I was a young lad. Nothing's made to last now, nothing's made to last! We pick our friends for the cars they drive, or the clothes they wear, or for some society they belong to. Oh, people aren't valued the way they were years ago; then a person was valued for what he was good for, his good character and his honesty.

Oh, it's quite a problem now for young people with great big high educations. I tell my grandchildren, "Learn to use your hands! That's something nobody can steal from you. Learn everything you possibly can; that's yours!" It's not like giving them money, you know.

I have three questions I like to ask people: "What is success?" Everybody has a different answer. One of the presidents of the United States, maybe it was Lincoln, once said, "Success is the way a person gets along with people in his own community." Another is: "What is time?" The third question is: "What is education?" And you know everybody defines them differently. You know, a lot of people say they can't do something. Somebody said, "Pat, can you play the fiddle?" and Pat said, "Well, by jiggers, I don't know, I never th'ried!" Now, isn't that worth thinking about?

Oh, they got along, the old people got along! George Bernard Shaw said one time, "People are always blaming their circumstances for what they are. I don't believe in circumstances. The people who get on in this world are the people who get up and look for the circumstances they want, and if they can't find them, make them!" And there's a lot in that. I've seen some people who said, "Oh, I've tried that and oh, it just didn't turn out," and I tell them, "Lookit! You haven't as much ambition as you had when you were sixteen months old! When you tried to get up and fell down then, if you'd said, 'I'm through,' you'd be sitting on the floor yet! You fell and got up, fell and got up, fell and got up..." Now is that right or wrong?

I've been sixty-seven years blacksmithing and I'm at it yet. It's like the old fellow with the red nose; when somebody asked him, "What's that red nose for?" he said, "I don't know, it's not finished yet!"

Oh, I've seen a lot, seen a lot in eighty-four years and I've enjoyed it. A wise man once said, "Your life is like your bank account; you've got to put something into it before you can get anything out of it." Isn't that true?

I have a great time watching people when I go to talk to groups in the city. I never saw so many sad faces in all my life as I have in these crowds from the city. I'll say to my grandson, Brett: "You watch for the sourest, saddest-looking face and I'll make her laugh!" They come along, maybe half-a-dozen together, and there'll be one, you'd just think she'd dropped in to get a butcher knife to go home and kill her mother-in-law; just terrible! And I step up to her quietly and say, "Lookit, have you got any notion of learning the blacksmithing?" Oh, she'll jump backwards three or four feet. "Me? Learn the blacksmithing?" And I say, "Yes, if you and some of you younger people don't take it up, it's going to go out altogether!" And, lookit, in two minutes I have her laughing!

I enjoy company but I'm never lonely; I guess I could say now my best friend is meditation; I do like to meditate. I tell people I don't want to be known as the richest man in the world but I would like to know there will be a lot of friends at my wake and funeral. There's an old saying I often think about: "From the day you are born till you leave in a hearse, anything that happens could always be worse!" Sometimes I think that none of us are thankful enough for our health and everything we have; we still find something to grumble about. I heard a little story years ago and it went something like this: "If we all had the opportunity to go to the marketplace in the town where we live, put our lot down and walk around and look at everybody else's lot, most likely we'd come back, pick up our own and go home happy."

You know, as you get older and living alone — I've been living alone for nearly twenty years — you live with your memories a great deal. I like to think back to the days when there were still seven days in the week; now it seems there's just washday and Saturday. There's so much going on and everybody rushing around. I was talking to a friend, Johnny Scott one day about that. John was born in Italy and when he came to this country he brought a lot of good ideas and wisdom with him and he really got along well. He's a very popular man all over the country and we were talking about the way things have changed. "Everybody now, they just go rip-a-tear!" he said and could you ever get a better expression if you looked for a month?

Oh, we're all in such a hurry we hardly take time to live. You know, a lot of people think about death a lot, especially the young people, but as you get older you realize death is only another part of life. Oh, people have to take time to think, time to remember. I like to remember the tough times and I like to remember the good times.

When I'm talking to a bunch of people I tell them I'm glad they asked me to talk on blacksmithing. I like to talk about blacksmithing, I like to talk about my hobbies and I like to talk about my family. I remember what Mahatma Gandhi, the old leader in India, once said: "My life is my message." One time, when I was reciting "The Village Blacksmith" — I nearly always recite that for a crowd — there was a really old lady at the back. She had a lovely face. "My life is my message" was written right there on her face and she said every word to herself. *My* life is *my* message; blacksmithing is my message.

In 1955 Graham took his mother and me to Vermont to visit some cousins, then we drove on to Boston and we found out that Boston is a place where you meet yourself coming and going so we took bus tours around the city. One of these tours took us to Henry Wadsworth Longfellow's home where the old poem, "The Village Blacksmith," was written. Well, it so happened that I walked in there on the hundredth anniversary to the hour of the day that Longfellow wrote that poem. Now, wasn't that strange? I was loaded down with blacksmithing; my father learned his trade from his brother, a blacksmith and my mother's brother, William Wrathall, learned with my father. I learned with my father and I had six or seven apprentices.

Anyway, the guide showed us Longfellow's desk where he had sat writing his poems and the place at the other side of the room where he used to stand up when he was composing. Now, wasn't it great for me to see that? I always liked that poem; it was in our school reader and I couldn't wait for the teacher to go over that with us. I use it a lot when I'm talking to groups of people and a lot of them remember it.

The closer you get to ninety, the younger ninety seems to be; it doesn't take long to put in a hundred years now. Oh, things are going pretty fast now, going too fast for me, but there's going to be an awful lot lost when our bunch go, information that we've learned the hard way. My life has been full of challenges right through and the one I'm facing now is old age and I want to meet it head on! You know I read somewhere, "You're as old as your doubts and as young as your hopes!" You know there's some people die at seventeen and don't get buried until they're seventy-five.

I often think of the old quotation: "When you are young, you should keep company with the old; when you are old, keep company with the young." That way you'll never get too far to one side, you know.